NEANDERTHALS: OUR CLOSEST RELATIVES

By Rayan Darcy

Origins: The Evolution of Homo Species Series

Book 5\6

Table of Contents

Introduction

Welcome to "Neanderthals: Our Closest Relatives" the fifth book in our series exploring the fascinating journey of human evolution. If you haven't read the first four books, "Homo habilis: The Handy Man," "Homo erectus: The First Travelers," "Homo heidelbergensis: The Bridge to Modern Humans," and "Denisovans: The Ghosts of the Ancient World," we highly recommend starting there to gain a foundational understanding of the early members of the Genus Homo. Each of these books provides essential context for understanding the evolutionary advancements and adaptations that have shaped our species. However, if you are only interested in Neanderthals, this book will be enough.

In this book, we delve into the fascinating world of the Neanderthals, a group of our closest ancient relatives whose legacy continues to intrigue scientists and laypeople alike. Through examining their technological innovations, geographic dispersal, biological changes, and social structures, we aim to shed light on their significant contributions to human evolution. We'll explore their intelligence, their complex social behaviors, and their cultural achievements, which demonstrate their remarkable cognitive capabilities. Additionally, we will examine the nature of their interactions with Homo sapiens, including cooperation, competition, and interbreeding, to better understand our shared history. By grounding our narrative in scientific research, we ensure that this book is both realistic and engaging, providing a comprehensive view of how these ancient humans influenced the development of our species and the intricate web of connections that bind all human beings.

Book Organization

Chapter 1: Neanderthals Emerge:
This chapter delves into the discovery and initial understanding of the Neanderthals. We explore their emergence, the key fossil discoveries, and genetic analyses that have provided insight into this significant group of ancient humans. By examining the timeline and the significant sites where Neanderthal remains have been found, we lay the groundwork for understanding their place in human evolution.

Chapter 2: Physical Characteristics:
In this chapter, we examine the physical attributes of Neanderthals, including their cranial capacity, facial morphology, skeletal structure, and strength. We explore their robust builds, unique dental features, and what these traits reveal about their adaptations and lifestyle.

Chapter 3: Habitat and Environment:
We provide a detailed description of the climatic conditions, geography, flora, fauna, and available food resources in the habitats of Neanderthals. This chapter covers the diverse environments they inhabited across Europe and western Asia, and how they adapted to these regions.

Chapter 4: Tool Use and Technological Innovations:
This chapter explores the technological advancements of Neanderthals, focusing on their tool-making skills and use of fire. We compare their technological innovations with those of other contemporary hominins, highlighting their contributions to early human technology.

Chapter 5: Social Structure and Behavior:

 In this chapter, we explore the social structures and behaviors of Neanderthals, including their group dynamics, care for the sick and injured, and burial practices. We examine evidence of their communication methods, possibly including language, and their cultural expressions through art and symbolism.

Chapter 6: Interactions with Homo sapiens:

 This chapter examines the nature of interactions between Neanderthals and Homo sapiens, including evidence of cooperation, competition, interbreeding, and potential war. We explore how these interactions influenced the genetic and cultural evolution of both species.

Chapter 7: Interactions with Other Species:

 In this chapter, we discuss Neanderthals' interactions with other hominin species and animals in their environment. We explore their role as both hunters and prey, and how these interactions shaped their survival strategies and adaptations.

Chapter 8: A Story: The Cave Bear Encounter:

Using all that we have learned, we create a vivid narrative styled as both a novel and a documentary. We immerse you in a day in the life of a Neanderthal group, following them as they navigate the challenges of their environment. Experience their daily routines, social interactions, and how they fought a cave bear. Grounded in scientific research, this chapter ensures that the story is both realistic and enjoyable. This chapter will let you live among them, providing a deeply immersive experience.

Chapter 9: What If They Were Alive Today:
In this chapter, we explore the fascinating hypothetical scenario of Neanderthals living in the modern world. We discuss whether we would notice a Neanderthal among us. We also compare their intelligence to that of modern humans, examining how their cognitive abilities would measure up today. Additionally, we analyze which fields Neanderthals could potentially excel in, such as manual labor, craftsmanship, and possibly even certain aspects of science and technology, and which fields might be challenging for them. This chapter provides a thought-provoking look at how Neanderthals might adapt to and influence our world if they were alive today.

Chapter 10: Role in Human Evolution
This chapter explores the crucial role Neanderthals played in human evolution. We discuss their genetic contributions and their impact on early human societies, highlighting the interconnectedness of our evolutionary history.

Chapter 11: How They Became Extinct
In this chapter, we will discuss how Neanderthals became extinct and what role Homo sapiens may have played in their disappearance.

Each chapter in this book aims to provide a comprehensive understanding of Neanderthals. By the end of this journey, you will have a deeper appreciation of our cousins, the Neanderthals, and their significant contributions to human evolution.
To start, we need to go back to the very beginning of the Neanderthals' emergence, around 400,000 years ago.

CHAPTER I: NEANDERTHALS EMERGE

The Discovery in Neander Valley:

The discovery of Neanderthals' first fossil was a monumental event in the history of paleoanthropology, marking a significant leap in our understanding of human evolution. This journey began in the Neander Valley near Düsseldorf, Germany. However, before the renowned 1856 discovery, there were earlier finds that went unrecognized. In 1829, a partial child's skull was found in Engis, Belgium, and in 1848, a skull was discovered in Forbes' Quarry in Gibraltar. Both were initially thought to belong to Homo sapiens. The significant breakthrough came in 1856 when limestone quarry workers uncovered skeletal remains in the Neander Valley. Johann Carl Fuhlrott, a local schoolteacher and natural historian, was the first to recognize the importance of the find. When he examined the remains, which included a skullcap, femur, and arm bones, he was struck by their unusual characteristics. The skull was low and elongated, with a prominent brow ridge and large eye sockets, features that starkly contrasted with those of modern humans. Fuhlrott's observations led him to propose that these bones belonged to an ancient, more primitive form of human. However, many scientists initially believed these bones belonged to a modern human with a disease or deformity.

Fuhlrott's initial interpretation faced significant skepticism and controversy. At the time, the prevailing scientific view did not readily accept the existence of human ancestors significantly different from modern Homo sapiens. The idea of evolution itself, though gaining traction through the work of Charles Darwin and others, was still hotly debated. It was Hermann Schaaffhausen, a professor of anatomy at the University of

Bonn, who supported Fuhlrott's assertion. Schaaffhausen published a detailed analysis of the Neander Valley remains, emphasizing their distinct anatomical features and arguing that they represented a different and ancient human form. This analysis laid the groundwork for a more systematic study of the fossils. The first scientist to formally suggest that these remains represented a separate species was William King, an Irish geologist. In 1864, King presented his findings to the British Association for the Advancement of Science. He proposed the name Homo neanderthalensis, honoring the site of their discovery. King's proposal marked a pivotal moment in paleoanthropology, as it was the first time a fossil hominin was classified as a distinct species separate from modern humans. This classification sparked considerable debate within the scientific community, with some researchers arguing that Neanderthals were simply an archaic variety of Homo sapiens, while others contended they were a completely different species.

Timeline and Existence:

Neanderthals are believed to have first appeared around 400,000 years ago. Their range was extensive, covering much of Europe, the Middle East, and western Asia. Unlike Homo sapiens and some other hominin species, Neanderthals did not emerge in Africa. Like the Denisovans, Neanderthals are thought to have originated outside Africa, specifically in Europe and western Asia. Fossils and archaeological evidence suggest that Neanderthals thrived in diverse environments, from the cold tundras of northern Europe to the warmer Mediterranean regions. They were highly adaptable, with physical and cultural traits that enabled them to survive in varying climates and terrains. The robust build of Neanderthals, characterized by their thick bones and muscular bodies, was well-suited to the harsh conditions of the Ice Age. Despite the significant differences between Neanderthals and modern humans, there is ongoing debate about their relationship to Homo sapiens. Some researchers consider Neanderthals to be a distinct species, Homo neanderthalensis, while others argue that they were a subspecies of Homo sapiens, referring to them as Homo sapiens neanderthalensis. This latter view is supported by evidence of interbreeding between Neanderthals and early modern humans. Genetic studies have shown that non-African modern human populations carry approximately 1-2% Neanderthal DNA, indicating that interbreeding occurred when the two groups coexisted in Europe and Asia.

The Impact on Human Evolution Studies:

The discovery of Neanderthals has had a profound and lasting impact on the field of human evolution studies, reshaping our understanding of what it means to be human and challenging long-held assumptions about our unique place in the natural world. The recognition of Neanderthals as a distinct species—or at the very least a significant subspecies—has opened up new avenues of research and prompted a re-evaluation of many aspects of human evolution. This pivotal finding has led to the identification of more than 20 different Homo species, significantly expanding our knowledge of the human family tree and highlighting the diversity of our ancient relatives. These discoveries have helped answer many questions about human origins, adaptation, and migration, showing that the evolutionary history of humans is far more complex than previously thought. One of the key insights gained from the study of Neanderthals is the realization that Homo sapiens were not alone in the world; we had several close relatives, or "cousins," who shared the planet with us at various points in history. This has fundamentally altered our understanding of human evolution, emphasizing that it was not a straightforward, linear process but rather a rich tapestry of interactions and coexistence among different hominin species. The evidence of interbreeding between Homo sapiens and Neanderthals, as well as with other hominins like Denisovans, underscores the interconnectedness of these groups and the genetic legacy they have left in modern human populations.

The Neanderthal discoveries have also underscored the importance of interdisciplinary approaches in studying human evolution. By integrating data from archaeology, genetics, anthropology, and other fields, scientists have been able to construct a more comprehensive and nuanced picture of our ancient past. This holistic approach has not only enhanced our understanding of Neanderthals but has also provided valuable insights into the broader patterns and processes that have shaped human evolution. As a result, the study of Neanderthals and other ancient hominins continues to be a dynamic and evolving field, driving new research and discoveries that further enrich our knowledge of human history. The realization that we shared the planet with other hominin species has fundamentally changed the narrative of human uniqueness, highlighting a history of shared heritage and continuous interaction. This understanding not only deepens our appreciation of the complexity of human evolution but also emphasizes the importance of preserving and studying our ancient past to uncover the mysteries of our origins and the evolutionary journey that has led to the emergence of Homo sapiens.

Ongoing Research:

Ongoing research into Neanderthals continues to reveal fascinating insights into their lives and their interactions with other hominin species. Advances in technology, such as more precise dating methods and sophisticated genetic analysis, are allowing scientists to piece together a more detailed and accurate picture of Neanderthal existence. Recent studies have focused on understanding their diet, social structures, and the reasons behind their eventual extinction. Researchers are also exploring the extent and nature of Neanderthal contributions to the modern human gene pool, shedding light on how interbreeding has influenced contemporary human traits. Collaborative efforts across various scientific disciplines are critical in this endeavor, enabling a more integrated approach to studying the past. These ongoing investigations not only deepen our knowledge of Neanderthals but also enhance our understanding of human resilience and adaptation in the face of changing environments and challenges. As the field of paleoanthropology progresses, each new discovery adds another piece to the complex puzzle of human evolution, reinforcing the interconnectedness of all human species and the shared history that binds us together.

CHAPTER 2:
PHYSICAL CHARACTERISTICS

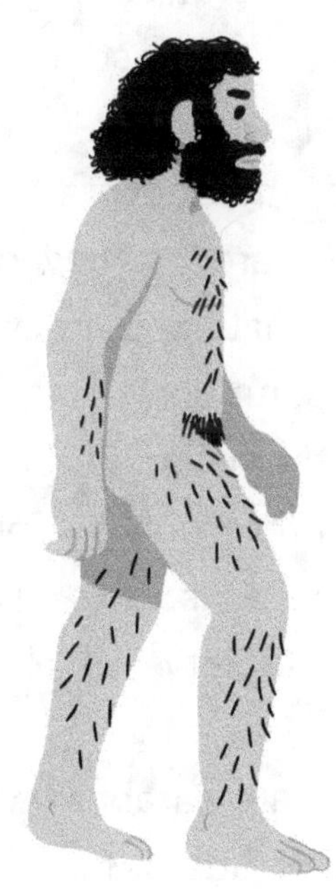

Neanderthals were a distinct species with unique physical characteristics that set them apart from both their ancient contemporaries and modern humans. Understanding these traits provides valuable insights into their adaptations to the environments they inhabited, their daily lives, and their interactions with other species, including Homo sapiens. This chapter delves into the various aspects of Neanderthal physicality, comparing them to modern humans to highlight the similarities and differences that define our ancient relatives.

Skin, Hair, and Eye Color:

Neanderthals displayed a range of skin, hair, and eye colors, influenced by their adaptation to varying climates across Europe and western Asia. Genetic studies suggest that Neanderthals had a diverse appearance, with some individuals possessing light skin, red or blond hair, and light-colored eyes—adaptations that likely helped them synthesize vitamin D in regions with low sunlight. These traits are believed to have evolved independently in Neanderthals and modern humans, illustrating parallel evolutionary solutions to similar environmental challenges. In contrast, other Neanderthals may have had darker skin and hair, providing protection against the sun's ultraviolet rays in more temperate regions. This diversity in pigmentation demonstrates the adaptability of Neanderthals to their environments. When compared to modern humans, Neanderthals' physical appearance was similarly varied, reflecting a wide range of adaptations to different ecological niches. The genetic evidence of interbreeding between Neanderthals and early modern humans indicates that some of these traits may have been passed down, contributing to the genetic diversity seen in contemporary human populations. This interbreeding has left a lasting legacy in modern humans, influencing various traits related to skin, hair, and immune responses. Additionally, the diversity in Neanderthal appearance challenges the simplistic view of them as a homogenous group, highlighting the complexity of their adaptation to different environments and climates. Their ability to adapt to varying levels of UV radiation and dietary sources of vitamin D showcases their evolutionary flexibility and resilience. The range of Neanderthal pigmentation also suggests that they occupied a variety of ecological niches, from dense forests to open plains, requiring different levels of melanin in their skin to protect against sun exposure while still allowing adequate vitamin D synthesis in less sunny regions. This variability in physical traits underscores the sophisticated evolutionary strategies that Neanderthals employed to thrive in a wide array of environmental conditions.

Body Hair and Physiological Traits:

 Neanderthals likely had more body hair than modern humans, a trait that would have provided additional insulation in the cold climates they often inhabited. This increased body hair, coupled with their robust physical build, suggests that Neanderthals were well-adapted to surviving harsh and variable temperatures. Their physiological traits also included a larger nasal cavity, which is believed to have helped warm and humidify the cold, dry air before it reached their lungs. These adaptations were crucial for maintaining body heat and respiratory health in Ice Age environments. Compared to modern humans, who generally have less body hair and more streamlined physiologies adapted to a wide range of climates, Neanderthals exhibit clear evolutionary responses to the cold. Additionally, their short limbs and stocky bodies reduced the surface area exposed to the cold, minimizing heat loss—a stark contrast to the longer limbs and leaner builds of many modern human populations that evolved in warmer climates. The body hair of Neanderthals likely played a significant role in their ability to conserve heat, working in conjunction with their dense musculature and robust skeletal structure to provide a natural barrier against the cold. These traits reflect a lifestyle that was highly dependent on physical strength and endurance, requiring substantial caloric intake and efficient thermal regulation. Neanderthals' physiological adaptations extend beyond their external characteristics, including metabolic adjustments that allowed them to thrive in resource-scarce environments. Their diet, rich in animal proteins and fats, supported their heavy musculature and high energy demands, while their physiological traits ensured they could extract maximum energy from their food and maintain body heat in freezing conditions. This comprehensive suite of adaptations underscores the evolutionary pressures Neanderthals faced and their remarkable ability to thrive in some of the most challenging environments of the Pleistocene epoch. Their physiological resilience is evident in the fossil record, which shows that Neanderthals could endure significant physical trauma and recover from injuries that would likely have been fatal for modern humans. This remarkable adaptability and physiological fortitude enabled Neanderthals to survive and prosper in environments that were often inhospitable and fluctuating.

Physical Build and Stature:

 Neanderthals were generally shorter but more robustly built than modern humans. On average, Neanderthal men stood about 5 feet 5 inches (165 cm) tall and weighed around 172-183 pounds (78-83 kg), while women were around 5 feet 1 inch (155 cm) tall and weighed about 139-146 pounds (63-66 kg). Their bones were thicker and denser, indicating a physically demanding lifestyle that required great strength and endurance. This robust build included wide hips, broad shoulders, and powerful muscles, which allowed Neanderthals to undertake the physically intensive tasks required for survival, such as hunting large game and processing animal hides. In comparison, modern humans tend to have a more gracile build, with longer limbs and a lighter frame, reflecting a different set of evolutionary pressures and adaptive strategies. The physical build of Neanderthals provided them with several advantages in their environment. Their shorter limbs and stockier bodies reduced the surface area exposed to the cold, helping to conserve heat, while their powerful musculature supported their active lifestyle. This build also indicates a high level of physical activity, as evidenced by the pronounced muscle attachments on their bones. These characteristics suggest that Neanderthals were well-suited for endurance activities, such as long-distance trekking and persistence hunting, which would have been essential for their survival. The denser bones of Neanderthals also suggest a higher level of physical resilience, enabling them to withstand the stresses and strains of their environment. This physical robustness is a testament to their adaptation to a life that was heavily reliant on physical strength and endurance.

Compared to modern humans, whose taller and more slender frames are adapted to a variety of climates and lifestyles, Neanderthals' physical build reflects a highly specialized adaptation to their specific ecological niche. Their physicality not only highlights the differences in lifestyle and environmental pressures between Neanderthals and modern humans but also underscores the evolutionary pathways that have shaped each species' unique characteristics. The robustness of Neanderthals' physical build is further emphasized by their ability to engage in close-quarter hunting techniques, often requiring direct confrontation with large and dangerous prey. This physical prowess was a key factor in their survival and success as a species. If we were to apply modern body mass index (BMI) calculations to Neanderthals, their weight relative to their height would classify many of them as overweight or even obese by today's standards. For example, a Neanderthal man standing 5 feet 5 inches tall and weighing 178 pounds would have a BMI of approximately 29.6, which is considered overweight. Similarly, a Neanderthal woman standing 5 feet 1 inch tall and weighing 143 pounds would have a BMI of approximately 27, also considered overweight. However, it is important to note that BMI does not account for muscle mass and bone density, both of which were significantly higher in Neanderthals compared to modern humans. Therefore, the classification of Neanderthals as overweight by contemporary BMI standards does not accurately reflect their physical health and fitness, which were well-suited to their environment and lifestyle.

Facial and Skull Structure:

Neanderthals had distinctive facial and skull structures that set them apart from modern humans. They had a pronounced brow ridge, a large, wide nose, and a forward-projecting face. Their skulls were elongated with a prominent occipital bun at the back. These features are thought to be adaptations to their environment, with the large nasal cavity helping to warm and humidify cold air and the robust facial structure providing support for powerful jaw muscles. The shape of their skulls also suggests a different brain organization compared to modern humans, and their brain size was larger on average. In comparison, modern humans have a more rounded skull, smaller brow ridges, and a flatter face, which are adaptations to a different set of environmental pressures and lifestyle changes. The facial structure of Neanderthals, with their prominent brow ridges and large noses, provided several functional advantages. The large nasal cavity, in particular, would have been beneficial for breathing in cold and dry environments, allowing the air to be warmed and humidified before reaching the lungs. This adaptation would have been crucial for maintaining respiratory health in the frigid climates of the Pleistocene epoch. Additionally, the robust facial bones and forward-projecting face suggest that Neanderthals had strong jaw muscles, which would have been advantageous for their diet, which likely included a significant amount of tough, fibrous plant material and meat. The occipital bun, a distinctive feature of Neanderthal skulls, provided a counterbalance for their large, heavy faces and may have also been related to their brain organization. Although Neanderthals had a larger brain size compared to modern humans, the shape and structure of their skulls indicate differences in brain development and function. These anatomical differences reflect the unique evolutionary paths taken by Neanderthals and modern humans, shaped by the distinct environments and lifestyles of each species. The robustness of their skulls and facial features underscores the physically demanding lifestyle of Neanderthals and their need for strong masticatory muscles to process a varied and often tough diet. This adaptation was crucial for their survival, allowing them to efficiently consume a wide range of food sources.

Brain Size, Intelligence, and Cognitive Capabilities:

Neanderthals had brains that were larger on average than those of modern humans, with brain sizes ranging from approximately 1,500 to 1,740 cubic centimeters (cc), compared to the average modern human brain size of about 1,350 cc. However, the shape of their brains differed, with Neanderthals having a more elongated braincase and a different organization of brain regions. This difference in brain structure suggests that while Neanderthals may have had similar cognitive capabilities to modern humans, they likely processed information and interacted with their environment in ways that were distinct. Neanderthals demonstrated advanced cognitive abilities, as evidenced by their use of complex tools, symbolic behavior, and possible use of language. However, their cognitive strengths may have differed from those of modern humans, potentially excelling in spatial awareness and physical problem-solving rather than abstract thinking. The similarities in brain size between Neanderthals and modern humans indicate that both species had the capacity for complex thought and social behavior. Neanderthals' cognitive capabilities are further supported by archaeological evidence of their use of tools, such as spears, scrapers, and awls, which required planning, skill, and an understanding of materials. The presence of symbolic artifacts, such as carved bones and shells, suggests that Neanderthals engaged in symbolic thought and possibly had a form of language. These cognitive abilities highlight the intelligence and adaptability of Neanderthals, challenging earlier perceptions of them as less advanced than modern humans. The differences in brain organization between Neanderthals and modern humans may have led to variations in cognitive strengths. Neanderthals' larger occipital lobes, for example, suggest that they may have had superior visual processing abilities, which would have been advantageous for hunting and navigating complex environments. In contrast, modern humans have larger parietal lobes, associated with abstract thinking and complex social interactions. These differences reflect the distinct evolutionary pressures faced by each species and the unique adaptations that arose as a result. The cognitive capabilities of Neanderthals, as evidenced by their sophisticated tool use and possible symbolic behavior, indicate a level of intelligence and adaptability that was crucial for their survival in challenging environments. This cognitive complexity is a testament to their evolutionary success and their ability to thrive in diverse and often harsh environments.

Strength and Endurance:

Neanderthals were incredibly strong and exhibited significant physical endurance, traits that were essential for their survival in the challenging environments of the Pleistocene. Their robust bones and powerful muscles indicate that Neanderthals were well-adapted to a physically demanding lifestyle that included hunting large game, gathering resources, and building shelters. The dense bone structure of Neanderthals provided the necessary support for their powerful muscles, enabling them to perform strenuous activities over extended periods. In comparison, modern humans generally have a more gracile build, with less muscle mass and bone density, reflecting a shift towards a lifestyle that relies less on physical strength and more on technological and social adaptations. The physical strength of Neanderthals is evident from the muscle attachment sites on their bones, which are much more pronounced than those of modern humans. These attachment sites indicate that Neanderthals had larger and more powerful muscles, particularly in the arms and legs, which would have been essential for tasks such as hunting, tool-making, and carrying heavy loads. Estimates suggest that Neanderthal men could bench press around 300-500 pounds, and women around 200-300 pounds. Their physical endurance is also suggested by their thick, dense bones, which would have been less prone to fractures and better able to withstand the stresses of a physically demanding lifestyle. This strength and endurance would have been crucial for Neanderthals' survival, allowing them to hunt large, dangerous animals and endure the harsh conditions of their environment. Compared to modern humans, Neanderthals' physical prowess highlights the evolutionary adaptations that enabled them to thrive in their specific ecological niche. While modern humans have developed different strategies for survival, such as advanced tools and social cooperation, the strength and endurance of Neanderthals reflect a direct and robust approach to interacting with their environment. These physical differences underscore the diverse paths of human evolution and the unique adaptations that have emerged in response to varying environmental pressures. The physical strength of Neanderthals, as evidenced by their robust skeletal structure and powerful musculature, highlights the evolutionary pressures they faced and their remarkable ability to thrive in some of the most challenging environments of the Pleistocene epoch. Their physical resilience and adaptability were key factors in their survival and success as a species.

In conclusion, Neanderthals were a uniquely adapted species with distinct physical characteristics that enabled them to thrive in a variety of challenging environments. Their diverse skin, hair, and eye colors, robust body hair and physiological traits, and powerful physical build all reflect their evolutionary responses to the harsh conditions of the Pleistocene epoch. The distinctive facial and skull structures of Neanderthals, along with their larger brain size and cognitive capabilities, highlight the complex interplay of factors that shaped their evolution. Additionally, their remarkable strength and endurance underscore their ability to survive and prosper in physically demanding environments. By comparing these traits to those of modern humans, we gain a deeper understanding of the diverse evolutionary pathways that have shaped our species and our ancient relatives.

CHAPTER 3: HABITAT AND ENVIRONMENT

Neanderthals lived in a wide range of environments across Europe and western Asia, adapting to various climates and landscapes. They inhabited diverse regions, including Europe and Asia, with unique geographical ranges and migration patterns. They had varied food sources and diets, utilized water sources and settlement patterns strategically, and faced numerous environmental challenges that required innovative survival strategies.

Europe: Habitats and Living Conditions:

In Europe, Neanderthals inhabited diverse environments, ranging from the cold, glacial landscapes of northern Europe to the more temperate regions of southern Europe. The harsh winters in northern Europe required significant adaptations, as temperatures could plummet to extreme lows, often below freezing for extended periods. Neanderthals developed robust physiques with large body fat reserves and thicker body hair, similar to that of the mammoth, which helped them retain body heat. Their stocky bodies and substantial fat layers acted as insulation, protecting them from the severe cold. They also made use of caves and rock shelters, which provided natural protection from the elements. These shelters not only offered warmth but also served as sites for social gatherings and tool-making activities. In southern Europe, where the climate was milder with temperatures varying between 10°C to 20°C, Neanderthals experienced a more diverse and abundant ecosystem. These regions were rich in vegetation and wildlife, offering a variety of food sources. The temperate climates allowed Neanderthals to exploit both plant and animal resources, contributing to a more varied diet. The presence of large rivers and lakes in parts of Europe facilitated their access to water and fish, integrating aquatic resources into their diet. This ability to include seafood, such as fish and mollusks, added essential nutrients and diversity to their diet. The diversity of European landscapes, from dense forests to open plains, provided Neanderthals with numerous opportunities to develop specialized tools and hunting strategies, further enhancing their ability to thrive in these regions. They crafted sophisticated stone tools adapted to different purposes, from hunting large game to processing plant materials. The European Neanderthals demonstrated a remarkable capacity to adapt to both the frigid conditions of the Ice Age and the relatively warmer interglacial periods, which demanded different survival strategies and resource utilization. This adaptability is also seen in their use of available materials for tool-making, which varied from region to region depending on the local resources. Their settlements in Europe reflect a strategic choice of locations that offered shelter and resources, often returning to the same sites seasonally or repeatedly over years. The adaptation to different environments in Europe not only highlights their survival skills but also their social and cultural complexity, as they developed various subsistence strategies and social behaviors to cope with the challenges posed by different European climates and terrains.

Asia: Habitats and Living Conditions:

In Asia, Neanderthals inhabited regions extending from the Middle East to the Altai Mountains in Siberia. The environments in these areas were equally diverse, ranging from arid deserts with temperatures soaring above 40°C to lush forests with moderate climates. In the Middle East, Neanderthals had to adapt to the arid conditions, finding ways to secure water and food in a challenging environment. They often settled near rivers and oases, which provided essential resources. The Altai Mountains presented a different set of challenges, with colder temperatures and rugged terrain requiring Neanderthals to adapt to harsher living conditions. In these mountainous regions, they utilized caves and rock shelters extensively, much like their European counterparts, to protect themselves from the elements and predators. The colder climates of the Altai region necessitated the development of specialized clothing and shelters to maintain body heat and ensure survival. The varying environments in Asia required Neanderthals to be highly adaptable, utilizing different strategies and tools to exploit the resources available to them. Their ability to inhabit such a wide range of environments demonstrates their resilience and versatility as a species, capable of thriving in both arid deserts and frigid mountainous regions. The adaptation strategies in Asia highlight their ingenious use of natural resources, creating tools that were specifically designed for the type of environment they lived in. Whether it was in the searing heat of the desert or the freezing cold of the mountains, Neanderthals showed a remarkable ability to adjust their living conditions, which included building sturdy shelters and developing clothing to protect against the elements. Their survival in these diverse climates showcases their capability to endure and innovate, ensuring their sustenance and protection through intelligent and adaptive strategies. Neanderthals in the Middle East faced the challenge of extreme heat and arid conditions, necessitating a deep understanding of water sources and efficient hunting techniques to sustain their communities. They often settled near reliable water sources like rivers and oases, which not only provided hydration but also attracted game and allowed for the gathering of edible plants. These areas became hubs of Neanderthal activity, with evidence of repeated habitation suggesting a strategic use of these critical resources. In contrast, the Altai Mountains required Neanderthals to develop methods to combat the cold, such as creating insulated clothing from animal hides and constructing robust shelters capable of withstanding harsh winter conditions. The varied landscapes of Asia, from the expansive deserts to the dense forests, demanded a wide range of survival tactics, illustrating the Neanderthals' impressive adaptability. Their ability to thrive in such different environments is a testament to their innovative spirit and resourcefulness, showcasing their profound connection to and understanding of their surroundings. This versatility in habitat adaptation reflects a sophisticated level of technological and cultural development, enabling Neanderthals to exploit a diverse array of ecological niches across Asia.

Geographical Range and Migration Patterns:

Neanderthals' geographical range extended across much of Europe and into western Asia, from the Iberian Peninsula in the west to the Altai Mountains in Siberia in the east. Their migration patterns were influenced by climatic changes and the availability of resources. During glacial periods, Neanderthals likely migrated southwards to escape the extreme cold, settling in more temperate areas where food and water were more accessible. As the climate warmed, they expanded their range northwards again. This pattern of movement allowed Neanderthals to exploit a variety of environments, from open grasslands and forests to mountainous regions. Their ability to adapt to different habitats is evident from the archaeological evidence of their settlements and the diverse tools they used, which were tailored to the specific conditions of their surroundings. This geographical flexibility highlights their ability to survive in both extreme cold and relatively mild climates, a testament to their adaptability and resilience. Their migrations were not random but likely followed seasonal patterns and the availability of resources, demonstrating their sophisticated understanding of their environment and their ability to plan and anticipate changes in their habitat. Neanderthals' strategic movements across vast territories reveal their advanced cognitive abilities in navigating and exploiting diverse landscapes, from fertile valleys to rugged highlands, ensuring their survival through keen adaptation and resource management.

Food Sources and Diet:

Neanderthals' diet varied significantly depending on their environment. In colder northern regions, they relied heavily on hunting large herbivores such as mammoths, woolly rhinoceroses, and reindeer. These animals provided not only meat but also fat, which was crucial for energy and insulation in harsh climates. The high protein and fat intake from these large game animals was vital for their survival, offering the necessary calories and nutrients to sustain their physically demanding lifestyle. Neanderthals also hunted smaller mammals, birds, and occasionally scavenged to maximize their use of available resources. In more temperate regions, Neanderthals' diet included a greater variety of plant foods, such as nuts, fruits, and tubers, alongside meat from smaller game like deer, wild boar, and other regional fauna. These plant foods provided essential vitamins and minerals, complementing their meat-heavy diet and contributing to a balanced nutritional intake. The availability of diverse plant foods in temperate climates allowed Neanderthals to gather and consume seasonal fruits and nuts, adding variety and necessary nutrients to their diet.

There is also evidence that some Neanderthal groups consumed a significant amount of seafood, particularly those living near coastal areas. Shellfish, fish, and marine mammals provided essential nutrients such as omega-3 fatty acids, which are believed to have contributed to their cognitive development and overall health. The inclusion of seafood in their diet demonstrates their ability to exploit a wide range of food sources and adapt to different environments. In some environments, Neanderthals adapted their diets to be primarily vegetarian, consuming a wide range of plant-based foods, while in other regions, they were predominantly carnivorous, relying mainly on animal resources. Neanderthals displayed remarkable dietary flexibility, processing and preparing different types of food using cooking and preservation methods that maximized their nutritional intake. This variety ensured they could thrive on both predominantly carnivorous and omnivorous diets depending on the availability of resources. Some Neanderthal groups even showed signs of specialized hunting techniques, targeting specific prey species abundant in their habitats, which required deep knowledge and strategic planning. This adaptability in diet is a testament to their survival skills, as they could sustain themselves in diverse environments, from icy tundras to lush woodlands, showcasing their resilience and ingenuity in making the most of their surroundings.

Neanderthals' ability to diversify their diet according to regional availability highlights their sophisticated understanding of their environment and their capability to exploit it for sustenance. This comprehensive dietary strategy, encompassing a range of plants, animals, and marine resources, underscores their evolutionary success and adaptability in the face of changing climates and habitats.

Water Sources and Settlement Patterns:

 Neanderthals typically settled near reliable water sources, such as rivers, lakes, and springs. These locations provided not only drinking water but also opportunities for fishing and access to plant resources. Settlement patterns suggest that Neanderthals favored caves and rock shelters for habitation, which offered natural protection from the elements and predators. These sites often show evidence of repeated use, indicating that Neanderthals returned to the same locations seasonally or over long periods. In open landscapes, they constructed temporary shelters using available materials such as wood, stone, and animal hides. The choice of settlement sites was strategic, taking into account the availability of resources and the need for safety and comfort. Their settlements were often located in areas that offered a strategic advantage, such as elevated positions with a clear view of the surrounding landscape, which allowed them to spot potential threats and opportunities for hunting. The proximity to water sources was crucial not only for hydration but also for the abundance of food resources these areas typically offered, including fish and waterfowl. Their ability to build and maintain shelters in diverse environments reflects their architectural skills and understanding of their habitats. These shelters varied from simple windbreaks to more complex structures that provided warmth and protection throughout the year. The strategic placement and construction of their settlements indicate a sophisticated level of planning and environmental awareness, ensuring that their communities could thrive in a variety of ecological settings.

Environmental Challenges and Survival Strategies:

Neanderthals faced numerous environmental challenges, including fluctuating climates, resource scarcity, and competition with other predators. Their survival strategies were diverse and adaptive, including the development of specialized tools, social cooperation, and innovative hunting techniques. The harsh conditions of the Pleistocene epoch, with its dramatic climatic shifts, required Neanderthals to be highly adaptable. Their physical adaptations, such as their robust builds and body fat similar to that of mammoths, were crucial for surviving cold environments. Social cooperation played a significant role in their survival, as group hunting and shared resources ensured that communities could thrive even in times of scarcity. Their technological innovations, such as the creation of specialized hunting tools and techniques for processing food, allowed them to maximize their use of available resources. Neanderthals' ability to exploit a wide range of environments, from dense forests to open plains, demonstrates their resilience and ingenuity. Their social structures likely included complex communication systems and coordinated efforts for hunting and gathering. Additionally, their use of fire for warmth, cooking, and protection against predators was a critical adaptation that improved their chances of survival in diverse habitats.

Neanderthals also demonstrated remarkable problem-solving skills and the ability to learn from their environment, adjusting their strategies as needed to cope with new challenges. These survival strategies underscore the Neanderthals' capacity for innovation and their deep understanding of their environments, which were key factors in their long-term resilience and success as a species. Their adaptability not only allowed them to endure the harsh conditions of their time but also to thrive in a variety of ecological niches, showcasing their ability to respond to environmental pressures with effective and creative solutions.

In conclusion, Neanderthals exhibited remarkable adaptability to a wide range of environments, from the glacial landscapes of Europe to the diverse terrains of Asia. Their ability to thrive in both cold and temperate climates, develop specialized tools and strategies, and adapt their diet based on available resources underscores their resilience. By understanding their varied habitats and survival strategies, we gain valuable insights into the evolutionary paths that enabled Neanderthals to survive and prosper in the challenging conditions of the Pleistocene epoch.

CHAPTER 4:
TOOL USE AND INNOVATION

Neanderthals were highly skilled toolmakers and innovators, developing a variety of tools and technologies that significantly enhanced their ability to survive in diverse and often harsh environments. This chapter explores their tool use and technological innovations, highlighting their ingenuity and adaptability.

Early Tools and Techniques:

Neanderthals are known for their sophisticated stone tools, which they crafted using a technique known as the Levallois method. This technique involved preparing a stone core and then striking flakes from it, which were then shaped into various tools. These tools included scrapers, points, and blades, which were used for a variety of purposes such as hunting, processing animal hides, and woodworking. The precision and skill required to produce these tools indicate a high level of cognitive ability and manual dexterity. Neanderthals also utilized organic materials such as bone, wood, and antler to create tools, further showcasing their ability to adapt and innovate with available resources. Their tool-making skills were not limited to stone; they demonstrated an understanding of different materials' properties and how to best utilize them for their needs. The diversity in their toolkit reflects their ability to adapt to various environments and challenges, whether it was hunting large game in the open plains or processing plant materials in forested areas. This technological sophistication indicates that Neanderthals had a deep understanding of their environment and the resources available to them, allowing them to create effective tools for survival and everyday use. Their early tools and techniques represent a significant leap in human cognitive and cultural evolution, highlighting their innovative spirit and adaptability in the face of diverse and often challenging environments.

Hunting and Food Processing Tools:

Neanderthals developed a range of tools specifically designed for hunting and processing food. Their toolkit included spears, which were used for hunting large game animals. These spears were often hafted, meaning that a stone point was attached to a wooden shaft, creating a more effective hunting weapon. Evidence suggests that Neanderthals engaged in close-range hunting, indicating their physical prowess and bravery. Additionally, they used tools such as scrapers, knives, and saws for butchering animals, processing hides, and preparing food. Scrapers were essential for cleaning animal hides, making them suitable for clothing and shelter construction, while saws were used to cut through bone and wood efficiently. The efficiency and effectiveness of these tools played a crucial role in their ability to sustain themselves and their communities. The development of specialized hunting tools allowed Neanderthals to exploit a wide range of prey, from large herbivores like mammoths to smaller animals and birds. Their ability to create and use these tools effectively demonstrates their ingenuity and adaptability in various hunting scenarios. These tools also facilitated the processing of animal hides into clothing and shelters, essential for survival in harsh climates. The technological advancements in hunting and food processing tools reflect Neanderthals' deep understanding of their environment and their ability to innovate in response to changing conditions and challenges. This adaptability in tool use was critical to their survival and success as a species, showcasing their advanced cognitive abilities and strategic planning.

and cultural evolution, highlighting their innovative spirit and adaptability in the face of diverse and often challenging environments.

Hunting and Food Processing Tools:

Neanderthals developed a range of tools specifically designed for hunting and processing food. Their toolkit included spears, which were used for hunting large game animals. These spears were often hafted, meaning that a stone point was attached to a wooden shaft, creating a more effective hunting weapon. Evidence suggests that Neanderthals engaged in close-range hunting, indicating their physical prowess and bravery. Additionally, they used tools such as scrapers, knives, and saws for butchering animals, processing hides, and preparing food. Scrapers were essential for cleaning animal hides, making them suitable for clothing and shelter construction, while saws were used to cut through bone and wood efficiently. The efficiency and effectiveness of these tools played a crucial role in their ability to sustain themselves and their communities. The development of specialized hunting tools allowed Neanderthals to exploit a wide range of prey, from large herbivores like mammoths to smaller animals and birds. Their ability to create and use these tools effectively demonstrates their ingenuity and adaptability in various hunting scenarios. These tools also facilitated the processing of animal hides into clothing and shelters, essential for survival in harsh climates. The technological advancements in hunting and food processing tools reflect Neanderthals' deep understanding of their environment and their ability to innovate in response to changing conditions and challenges. This adaptability in tool use was critical to their survival and success as a species, showcasing their advanced cognitive abilities and strategic planning.

Fishing Tools and Techniques:

Neanderthals developed a variety of tools and techniques to fish and hunt marine animals, showcasing their ingenuity and adaptability. They likely used spears, nets, and traps to catch fish and other aquatic creatures. Spearfishing, in particular, would have been a common method, allowing Neanderthals to target fish in rivers, lakes, and coastal areas. These spears, often made from wood with sharpened points or stone tips, were effective for catching fish in shallow waters. Additionally, Neanderthals might have used nets woven from plant fibers to trap fish, indicating their understanding of fishing methods that required more complex planning and execution. Evidence from sites like the Figueira Brava in Portugal reveals that Neanderthals consumed a variety of fish species, including both freshwater and marine fish. The remains of fish bones and scales found in hearths suggest that fish were an important part of their diet, providing essential nutrients crucial for their health and development. This dietary inclusion of fish not only highlights their adaptability in utilizing available resources but also their ability to process and cook these resources effectively. Moreover, Neanderthals did not limit their aquatic hunting to fish; they also hunted larger marine animals such as seals and dolphins. Evidence suggests that they used coordinated group strategies to hunt these animals, which would have required significant planning and cooperation. The presence of marine mammal bones at various Neanderthal sites indicates that these larger sea animals were a valuable food source. Hunting marine mammals would have provided not only meat but also blubber and other materials that could be used for various purposes. The techniques used to hunt these larger animals likely included the use of more robust spears and possibly traps or ambush tactics near coastal areas. The ability to hunt both fish and larger marine animals demonstrates Neanderthals' advanced hunting skills and their capacity to exploit a wide range of ecological niches.

Evidence of Sailing:

The possibility that Neanderthals engaged in early forms of seafaring is supported by evidence suggesting they might have crossed water bodies that would have required some form of watercraft. Archaeological finds, such as those on the Greek islands of Crete and Naxos, indicate that Neanderthals or other early humans may have traveled across the Mediterranean Sea. These islands were never connected to the mainland, implying that early humans must have used boats or rafts to reach them. Although there is no direct evidence of Neanderthal boats, the presence of their artifacts on these islands strongly suggests that they had the capability to build and use watercraft. This would have required not only the construction of boats or rafts but also knowledge of navigation and the ability to manage the risks associated with open water travel. Further support for Neanderthal seafaring comes from the discovery of tools and bones on other isolated islands, which indicates repeated crossings and possibly established routes. The technological and cognitive skills required for such feats highlight Neanderthals' advanced capabilities and their innovative spirit. If Neanderthals did indeed engage in seafaring, it would signify a remarkable level of sophistication in their use of technology and understanding of their environment, enabling them to explore and exploit new territories. This potential for early seafaring adds another layer to our understanding of Neanderthals, demonstrating their versatility and adaptability in a variety of environments, including the challenging conditions of maritime navigation.

Starting Fire:

The ability to control fire was a critical technological innovation for Neanderthals, providing warmth, protection, and a means to cook food. However, whether Neanderthals could start fire themselves remains a topic of debate among researchers. There is strong evidence that they used fire extensively, as numerous hearths and burn marks on bones and tools have been found at Neanderthal sites. Fire allowed them to inhabit colder regions and survive harsh winters by providing necessary warmth and enabling the cooking of food, which made it more palatable and increased its nutritional value. Some researchers argue that Neanderthals may have been able to start fires using techniques similar to those employed by early Homo sapiens, such as striking flint against pyrite or using friction-based methods. Others suggest that they may have relied on natural sources of fire, such as lightning strikes, and maintained these fires for extended periods. As you might have observed in the third book of this series, "Homo Heidelbergensis: The Bridge to Modern Humans," I portrayed Neanderthals as capable of starting a fire in the story chapter. This depiction reflects my belief that they shared with us the ability to create fire. However, this remains speculative, and the true extent of their fire-starting abilities is still under investigation. Despite this uncertainty, the evidence of their extensive use of fire indicates a sophisticated understanding of its benefits and applications, whether they were starting it themselves or maintaining natural fires.

Clothing and Fabric Use:

Neanderthals demonstrated remarkable ingenuity in creating clothing to protect themselves from the harsh climates they inhabited. Evidence suggests that they used animal hides to make garments, which provided essential insulation against the cold. These garments likely included shoes, hats, and cloaks, designed to cover most of their bodies and retain body heat. The creation of clothing was not just about warmth but also about survival, as it enabled Neanderthals to hunt and gather in frigid environments without succumbing to hypothermia. Some archaeological finds indicate that Neanderthals may have used simple sewing techniques to stitch together pieces of hide, creating more effective and durable clothing. The use of bone needles and awls supports this idea, showing their ability to manipulate materials with precision. Additionally, recent discoveries suggest that Neanderthals might have used natural fibers to make simple fabrics, further enhancing their clothing and potentially their shelters. This technological innovation highlights their adaptability and resourcefulness, allowing them to thrive in environments where exposed skin would be vulnerable to frostbite and other cold-related injuries. The development and use of clothing and fabric underscore Neanderthals' advanced cognitive abilities and their capacity for innovation in response to environmental challenges.

Shelters and Their Construction:

Neanderthals were adept at constructing shelters that provided protection from the elements and predators. They used a variety of materials, including wood, stone, and animal bones, to build sturdy structures. One of the most fascinating discoveries is a Neanderthal shelter made from mammoth bones found at the site of Molodova in Ukraine. This shelter was constructed using large mammoth bones arranged in a circular pattern, covered with hides, and possibly insulated with additional materials. Such ingenuity in using available resources demonstrates their ability to adapt to their environment and create durable living spaces. These shelters provided necessary warmth and safety, especially in colder regions, and allowed Neanderthals to establish semi-permanent settlements. The use of mammoth bones and other durable materials in construction also highlights their resourcefulness and understanding of structural stability. Neanderthals' construction techniques varied depending on the region and available materials, showcasing their ability to innovate and adapt their building practices to different environmental challenges.

Technological Innovations and Adaptations:

 Neanderthals continually adapted their tool-making techniques to meet the demands of their changing environments. The development of specialized tools for specific tasks, such as hunting particular animals or processing different materials, showcases their ability to innovate and solve problems. Their technological advancements were not static but evolved over time, reflecting their ongoing adaptation to new challenges and opportunities. The ability to create and use a wide range of tools was a key factor in their survival, enabling them to efficiently exploit available resources. Neanderthals' technological innovations extended beyond simple tool use; they demonstrated a sophisticated understanding of materials and their properties, which allowed them to create more effective tools and improve their quality of life. This continuous evolution of technology indicates a dynamic culture capable of learning and adapting over generations. Their innovations were crucial for their survival, providing them with the means to hunt more effectively, process food, create clothing, and protect themselves from the elements. The technological prowess of Neanderthals highlights their ingenuity and resilience, showcasing their ability to adapt and thrive in diverse and often challenging environments.

In conclusion, Neanderthals' technological innovations and tool use were pivotal in their ability to adapt and thrive in diverse environments. From sophisticated stone tools and hunting weapons to the use of fire, clothing, and innovative shelters, Neanderthals demonstrated a remarkable capacity for innovation and problem-solving. Their technological advancements reflect their cognitive abilities and adaptability, providing insights into their daily lives and survival strategies. By studying these innovations, we gain a deeper understanding of how Neanderthals navigated their world, highlighting the complex interplay between environment, technology, and human evolution.

CHAPTER 5:

SOCIAL STRUCTURE AND BEHAVIOR

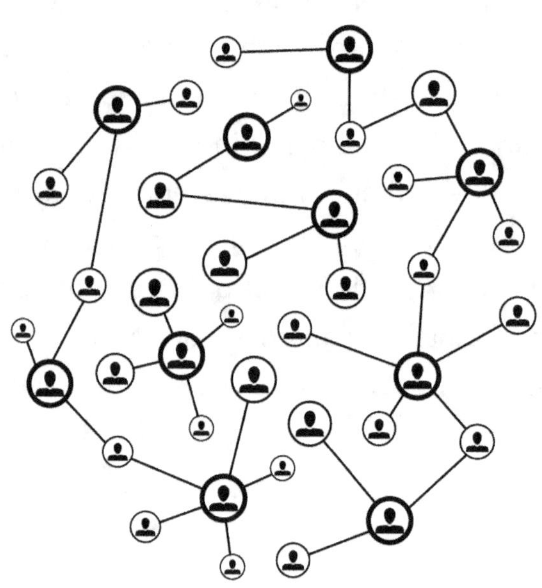

Neanderthals exhibited a complex social structure and behavior that included family-oriented groups, advanced medical knowledge, potential verbal communication, cultural expressions, and even practices like cannibalism. These aspects of their social life provide a deep understanding of their cognitive abilities and social dynamics, reflecting a sophisticated and adaptive species.

Group Size and Composition:

Neanderthals lived in small, close-knit groups typically consisting of 10 to 30 individuals. These groups were often based on extended family ties, including parents, children, grandparents, and possibly other relatives. This small group size facilitated strong social bonds and cooperation, essential for survival in their challenging environments. The close-knit nature of these groups allowed for efficient sharing of resources, coordinated hunting efforts, and collective care for the young and elderly. Living in such intimate social units required high levels of trust and mutual support, ensuring that all members contributed to the group's well-being. This familial structure also provided a framework for passing down important survival skills, such as tool-making, hunting strategies, and knowledge of medicinal plants, which were crucial for their continued survival in harsh and often changing climates. The intimate nature of their groups likely fostered deep emotional connections and a strong sense of identity and belonging, reinforcing the bonds that held these communities together. Moreover, the social dynamics within these groups would have involved complex interactions, including the division of labor, conflict resolution, and the establishment of social hierarchies, all of which were essential for maintaining group cohesion and stability.

Care for Group Members:

Neanderthals demonstrated a high level of care for their group members, including advanced medical knowledge and practices. Evidence from burial sites indicates that they tended to their sick and injured, with skeletal remains showing signs of healed injuries that would have required long-term care. For example, remains found at Shanidar Cave in Iraq show evidence of a male Neanderthal who survived multiple injuries, including a withered arm, a missing hand, and a crushed eye socket, all of which would have made independent survival unlikely. This suggests that his community must have provided him with consistent care and support, enabling him to live for many years despite his disabilities. Their knowledge of medicinal plants was likely comparable to early modern humans, allowing them to treat wounds and illnesses effectively. They might have used plants with anti-inflammatory, analgesic, and antibacterial properties, such as yarrow and chamomile, which were available in their environments. Neanderthals employed various techniques to treat injuries, such as setting broken bones and using plants with medicinal properties to alleviate pain and prevent infections. The discovery of dental plaque on Neanderthal teeth has revealed traces of medicinal plants, providing direct evidence of their use of natural remedies. The practice of burying their dead, often with grave goods, suggests a ritualistic aspect to their care for the deceased, reflecting a deep sense of community and respect for group members. This behavior indicates that Neanderthals might have had beliefs or rituals related to death and the afterlife, adding a spiritual dimension to their social care practices.

This compassionate behavior highlights their social cohesion and the importance of mutual support within their groups. The presence of healed injuries in elderly individuals further indicates that even those who were no longer able to contribute actively to the group's survival were cared for, showing a level of empathy and understanding that parallels modern human behavior. Such findings suggest that Neanderthal care extended beyond immediate family members to include all group members, fostering strong social bonds and a sense of belonging. The extensive care provided to the sick and injured would have required a significant investment of time and resources, underscoring the value placed on each individual within the group. Neanderthals' ability to provide such care suggests they had a deep understanding of medical practices and the use of natural resources to treat injuries and illnesses, underscoring their advanced cognitive abilities and their commitment to the well-being of their community members. This advanced level of care would have been crucial for the survival of individuals who could not have managed on their own, indicating a sophisticated level of social organization and empathy within Neanderthal communities. The evidence of such care practices provides insight into the complex social dynamics of Neanderthal groups, emphasizing their capacity for compassion and communal support, which were vital for their survival and cohesion as a species.

Communication and Language:

Similar to Denisovans, Neanderthals had the anatomical capability for speech, suggesting they could communicate verbally. The structure of their hyoid bone and the presence of the FOXP2 gene, associated with language and speech, indicate that they could produce a range of sounds necessary for complex communication. This ability would have been crucial for coordinating hunting efforts, sharing knowledge, and maintaining social bonds. Verbal communication likely played a significant role in their social dynamics, enabling them to transmit cultural knowledge and maintain group cohesion. The potential for complex language use among Neanderthals also suggests they had the cognitive capacity for abstract thought, planning, and social interaction, which are essential components of advanced social behavior. Their ability to communicate effectively would have facilitated the transmission of survival strategies, social norms, and cultural practices, ensuring the continuity and evolution of their communities over generations.

Learning and Cultural Transmission:

Neanderthals engaged in the transmission of cultural knowledge and skills across generations. While there is no definitive evidence of religion, the intentional burial of their dead and the inclusion of grave goods suggest a level of ritualistic behavior that could imply early forms of spiritual or symbolic thought. The process of learning and cultural transmission would have involved teaching young Neanderthals essential survival skills, such as tool-making, hunting techniques, and the use of medicinal plants. This transfer of knowledge ensured that each generation was equipped with the skills necessary to thrive in their environment. The presence of standardized tool types and evidence of complex social behaviors indicates that Neanderthals had established traditions and cultural norms that were passed down through generations. This ability to transmit knowledge and cultural practices highlights their cognitive sophistication and the importance of social learning in their communities.

Art and Cultural Expression:

Neanderthals exhibited significant cultural and symbolic behavior, including the creation of cave art and personal ornaments. They are the first species in history to produce symbolic representations, as evidenced by cave paintings found in Spain, which are attributed to Neanderthals. These paintings, consisting of red ochre dots and hand stencils, suggest an early form of symbolic thinking and cultural expression. The use of red ochre, a pigment made from iron oxide, indicates that Neanderthals had not only the cognitive ability to create art but also the technical skills to produce and apply these pigments. The choice of locations for these paintings, often in deep and dark parts of caves, suggests that these artworks held special significance and may have been part of ritualistic or communal activities. Additionally, Neanderthals created personal ornaments, such as beads made from animal teeth and shells, which were likely used for decorative or symbolic purposes. These ornaments indicate that Neanderthals engaged in practices of personal adornment and possibly conveyed social status, group identity, or individual accomplishments. The meticulous craftsmanship of these beads demonstrates their fine motor skills and aesthetic sensibility. The discovery of a flute-like instrument made from a bear bone indicates that they may have also engaged in musical activities. This instrument, with its carefully crafted holes, suggests that Neanderthals had an understanding of sound production and musical scales, adding another layer to their cultural complexity. Furthermore, the presence of engraved bones and stones, and the use of pigments for body and object decoration, imply a sophisticated level of symbolic thought. These artistic and cultural expressions reflect a high level of cognitive ability and an appreciation for aesthetics and symbolism, further underscoring their complexity as a species.

Cannibalism:

Evidence of cannibalism among Neanderthals has been found at several archaeological sites, indicating that they occasionally practiced this behavior. Skeletal remains with cut marks and signs of deliberate breakage suggest that Neanderthals sometimes consumed their dead, driven by nutritional needs during times of food scarcity or as part of ritualistic practices. Sites such as El Sidrón in Spain, Goyet in Belgium, and Moula-Guercy in France have provided clear evidence of butchery, including defleshing and marrow extraction. The presence of cannibalism underscores the harsh realities Neanderthals faced and their pragmatic approach to survival. However, this does not mean that all Neanderthals practiced cannibalism; most would likely have found it as repulsive as we do today. Additionally, cannibalism might have been an act of war or conflict, where consuming enemies could have been a way to assert dominance or as part of a ritualistic practice. Interestingly, early Homo sapiens exhibited similar rates of cannibalism, suggesting that it was a common adaptive strategy among early hominins in response to extreme conditions or as part of cultural practices. Understanding Neanderthal cannibalism provides valuable insights into their social dynamics and adaptability, reflecting their ability to utilize available resources while highlighting the diversity and complexity of their survival strategies. This practice, while unsettling from a modern perspective, emphasizes the challenging environments in which they lived and the lengths to which they went to survive.

In conclusion, Neanderthals displayed a complex social structure and behavior that included close-knit family groups, advanced medical knowledge—which was particularly important due to the frequent injuries they sustained from their hunting techniques—potential verbal communication, cultural expressions, and even cannibalism. These aspects of their social life highlight their cognitive abilities and adaptability, offering a glimpse into the rich and dynamic societies of our ancient relatives. By understanding their social structures and behaviors, we gain valuable insights into the evolutionary roots of human sociality and culture.

CHAPTER 6:

NEANDERTHALS AND HOMO SAPIENS

Neanderthals and Homo sapiens, two distinct human species, interacted in various ways as they encountered each other across different regions. Their interactions ranged from peaceful coexistence and cultural exchanges to conflict and competition, shaping the course of human evolution. This chapter delves into the complex relationship between these two species, exploring their first encounters, interbreeding, potential conflicts, and the eventual cooperation and exchange of experiences that enriched both cultures.

First Interactions:

The first interactions between Neanderthals and Homo sapiens likely occurred around 50,000 to 60,000 years ago in the Middle East. As modern humans migrated out of Africa, they encountered Neanderthals who had been living in Europe and parts of Asia for hundreds of thousands of years. Sites such as the Skhul and Qafzeh caves in Israel provide evidence of early modern humans and Neanderthals coexisting in the same regions, suggesting potential interactions. These encounters would have ranged from peaceful exchanges to competition for resources, setting the stage for a complex relationship between the two species. The archaeological record indicates that Neanderthals and Homo sapiens shared tools, techniques, and perhaps even ideas, leading to a fascinating blend of cultures and technologies. These interactions likely varied significantly depending on the region and circumstances, with some groups possibly engaging in mutual cooperation and others experiencing conflict and competition. The complexity of these early encounters set the stage for a dynamic and multifaceted relationship that would have profound implications for both species. Furthermore, the initial interactions may have included instances of trade, cultural exchanges, and intergroup marriages, creating a rich tapestry of shared knowledge and mutual influence. These first meetings would have been pivotal moments in human prehistory, shaping the cultural and genetic makeup of future generations. Over time, these interactions could have led to the development of shared territories and possibly even alliances, as both species sought to survive and thrive in their environments.

Interbreeding:

Interbreeding between Neanderthals and Homo sapiens is well-documented through genetic evidence. Modern humans across most of the world carry between 1% and 2% Neanderthal DNA, indicating that interbreeding occurred. This genetic mixing likely took place in multiple locations over tens of thousands of years as modern humans migrated into Neanderthal territories. The offspring of these unions, often referred to as hybrids, exhibited traits from both species, such as robust features inherited from Neanderthals combined with the more gracile features of Homo sapiens. These children likely had broader faces, larger noses, and more robust builds, paired with lighter skeletal frames and finer facial features. Genetically, these hybrids were fully capable of reproducing with either species, suggesting they could integrate into either Neanderthal or Homo sapiens communities. This integration would have been facilitated by their shared physical traits and abilities, making them versatile members of either group. The interbreeding process significantly contributed to the genetic diversity of modern humans and played a crucial role in the evolutionary trajectory of both species. The presence of Neanderthal DNA in modern humans has been linked to various physiological traits, such as enhanced immune system responses and adaptations to different environments. Neanderthal genes have been associated with better resistance to pathogens and the ability to adapt to colder climates, providing evolutionary advantages crucial for survival in diverse and changing environments. Additionally, the hybrids may have possessed cognitive and behavioral traits from both species, potentially benefiting from the cultural and technological knowledge of both Neanderthals and Homo sapiens. This genetic legacy highlights the profound impact of Neanderthal and Homo sapiens interactions on the development of human biology, showing how interbreeding helped shape the evolutionary paths of both species. The genetic contributions from Neanderthals may have provided Homo sapiens with certain advantages, such as resistance to pathogens and enhanced adaptation to colder climates, which were crucial for survival in diverse and changing environments. This genetic legacy highlights the profound impact of Neanderthal and Homo sapiens interactions on the development of human biology, demonstrating how interbreeding helped shape the evolutionary paths of both species and contributed to the diverse genetic makeup of modern human populations.

Forced Interbreeding:

The nature of interbreeding between Neanderthals and Homo sapiens raises questions about whether these encounters were always consensual. Some researchers suggest that interbreeding might have been a result of forceful encounters, potentially as an act of war or conflict. The power dynamics between the two species could have varied significantly depending on the context of their interactions. However, it is also possible that peaceful, consensual relationships contributed to the genetic mixing. The lack of definitive evidence makes it challenging to determine the exact nature of these interbreeding events, leaving room for multiple interpretations. It is believed that Neanderthal males more frequently mated with Homo sapiens females, which could reflect social or environmental factors influencing these interactions. Forced interbreeding, if it occurred, would have likely been driven by the same competitive and survival pressures that shaped other aspects of Neanderthal and Homo sapiens interactions. This aspect of their relationship underscores the complexity of their interactions, which ranged from cooperative to contentious. While it is important to acknowledge the potential for non-consensual encounters, it is equally important to consider the possibility of mutual attraction and alliance-forming that may have also played a role in these interspecies relationships.

Possible War:

The potential for conflict between Neanderthals and Homo sapiens is supported by archaeological evidence indicating violent encounters. Fossil records show signs of trauma, such as fractures and injuries caused by weapons, suggesting that some interactions were hostile. Sites like the Shanidar Cave in Iraq provide evidence of violent deaths, which could be attributed to interspecies conflict. These violent encounters might have been driven by competition for resources, territorial disputes, or cultural differences. The nature of warfare in prehistoric times was likely sporadic and opportunistic, rather than organized and prolonged. Conflicts would have arisen from direct competition over hunting grounds, shelter, and other critical resources, especially during periods of environmental stress. Defensive structures and fortifications at some sites imply strategic planning and tactical thinking, suggesting that confrontations were not merely spontaneous. The use of advanced weaponry, such as spears and possibly early forms of bows and arrows, indicates that these conflicts could have been quite deadly. Intense competition for resources, particularly during periods of climatic instability, would have exacerbated tensions, leading to more frequent and severe conflicts. Cultural differences, such as distinct social structures and belief systems, may have also played a role in these hostilities. The impact of these conflicts on social structures and survival strategies of both Neanderthals and Homo sapiens was significant. Frequent skirmishes would have led to a loss of life, disrupted social cohesion, and forced groups to adapt their strategies for survival. This might have included developing better weapons, forming larger, more cohesive groups for defense, or even migrating to avoid conflict zones. Overall, the evidence points to a complex and multifaceted relationship between Neanderthals and Homo sapiens, where cooperation and conflict coexisted. The occasional warfare or skirmishes between the two species highlight the competitive and sometimes violent nature of their interactions, driven by the need to secure resources and territory in a challenging and ever-changing environment. These conflicts likely shaped the evolutionary paths of both species, influencing their development and adaptation in significant ways.

Cooperation and Exchange of Experiences:

Despite the potential for conflict, there is also evidence of cooperation and cultural exchange between Neanderthals and Homo sapiens. Shared tool technologies and similar subsistence strategies indicate that both species learned from each other. Neanderthals adopted some aspects of Homo sapiens' tool-making techniques, such as the use of more refined stone tools and the development of composite tools that combined different materials for greater efficiency. Conversely, modern humans might have benefited from the survival strategies and knowledge of the Neanderthals, who had lived in the challenging environments of Europe and Asia for hundreds of thousands of years. This exchange of experiences would have enriched both cultures, enhancing their ability to adapt to changing environments. The blending of skills and knowledge from both species likely played a crucial role in their respective evolutionary paths, fostering a dynamic and interconnected prehistoric world. Evidence suggests that the cooperation extended to joint hunting expeditions, where the combined efforts and diverse techniques of both species would have increased their success rates. Shared living spaces have been discovered, indicating that Neanderthals and Homo sapiens cohabited certain areas, potentially sharing resources and responsibilities. There are even indications of communal child-rearing practices, which would reflect a complex web of social interactions and mutual support. The evidence of shared hearths and overlapping habitation sites suggests that Neanderthals and Homo sapiens were capable of forming mutually beneficial relationships, driven by the common goal of survival. These cooperative interactions may have facilitated the transmission of crucial survival skills, such as fire-making, advanced tool use, and intricate knowledge of the local flora and fauna, which would have been invaluable in navigating their harsh and unpredictable environments. This mutual learning and exchange not only helped in immediate survival but also contributed to the long-term evolutionary success of both species, as they adapted and thrived in a variety of environments. This intricate web of cooperation highlights the sophisticated social dynamics and adaptive strategies that characterized the interactions between Neanderthals and Homo sapiens, providing a deeper understanding of the shared human journey and the foundations of modern human societies.

In conclusion, the relationship between Neanderthals and Homo sapiens was multifaceted, encompassing both conflict and cooperation. The first interactions, interbreeding events, and possible instances of violence paint a complex picture of their coexistence. Through cooperation and cultural exchange, both species enriched their own survival strategies, leaving a lasting impact on the evolutionary history of modern humans. The legacy of these interactions is evident in the genetic and cultural makeup of contemporary human populations, underscoring the deep connections that bind us to our ancient relatives. The relationship between Neanderthals and Homo sapiens was just like ours today: there were conflicts and wars, cooperation, and love. Our relationship with Neanderthals was human.

CHAPTER 7: INTERACTIONS WITH OTHER SPECIES

In this chapter, we will explore the interactions between Neanderthals and other hominin species besides Homo sapiens, whom we have discussed extensively, and Denisovans, covered in the previous book. Additionally, we will delve into their interactions with various animals, focusing on those they hunted, those that hunted them, and other unique or extinct species they coexisted with. This comprehensive examination will provide a detailed understanding of Neanderthal life and their ecological and social environments.

Interactions with Other Homo Species:

Neanderthals, alongside Homo sapiens and Denisovans, coexisted with several other hominin species during the Pleistocene epoch. One notable species is Homo heidelbergensis, considered a common ancestor of Neanderthals, Denisovans, and modern humans. Fossil evidence suggests that Homo heidelbergensis populations in Europe evolved into Neanderthals, while those in Africa contributed to the lineage of Homo sapiens, and those in Asia likely contributed to the lineage of Denisovans. Homo heidelbergensis is characterized by a mix of primitive and advanced traits, such as a large braincase and robust build, similar to both Neanderthals and modern humans. Although direct interactions between Neanderthals and Homo heidelbergensis are not well-documented, the transitional fossils and shared traits indicate a significant evolutionary relationship. The coexistence of these species in Europe would have involved shared habitats and possibly competition for resources, influencing their respective adaptations and evolutionary paths. Neanderthals, inheriting the advanced hunting strategies and tool-making skills of Homo heidelbergensis, likely further developed these techniques to suit their specific environments, thus contributing to their survival and evolutionary success.

Another prominent species is Homo erectus, an earlier hominin that spread across Africa, Asia, and Europe. Homo erectus is known for its advanced tool-making techniques, including the development of the Acheulean hand axe, and its long-term survival over nearly two million years. The overlap in timelines and geographic ranges of Homo erectus and Neanderthals suggests potential encounters, although specific evidence of direct interactions is scarce. The presence of Homo erectus in regions later inhabited by Neanderthals implies that the latter might have inherited or been influenced by their technological advancements and survival strategies. The evolutionary pressure exerted by coexisting with Homo erectus could have driven Neanderthals to refine their tools and hunting methods, contributing to their own technological sophistication. This influence would have been particularly evident in regions where the habitats of Homo erectus and Neanderthals overlapped, leading to a transfer of knowledge and skills that were crucial for adapting to changing environments and diverse ecosystems.

Additionally, there is evidence suggesting that Neanderthals might have encountered other hominins like Homo naledi and Homo floresiensis. Homo naledi, discovered in South Africa, represents a unique evolutionary branch with distinct physical and cultural traits, including a combination of primitive features and more advanced characteristics such as small, modern-like teeth and hands adapted for tool use. While direct evidence of interactions between Neanderthals and Homo naledi is limited, the possibility of contact opens intriguing questions about the extent of hominin diversity and interspecies relationships during the Pleistocene. Similarly, Homo floresiensis, found in Indonesia and often referred to as the "Hobbit" due to its small stature, represents another unique lineage. The potential for Neanderthal interactions with Homo floresiensis, though speculative, underscores the remarkable diversity of the Homo genus and the complex web of evolutionary interactions that shaped the development of these species. The existence of such diverse hominin species during the Pleistocene suggests a dynamic and competitive environment, where different species adapted to their specific niches while occasionally coming into contact and possibly exchanging knowledge and survival strategies.

These interactions, whether direct or indirect, highlight the complex web of hominin coexistence and evolutionary interplay that shaped the development of Neanderthals and other species within the Homo genus. The shared evolutionary heritage and the potential for interspecies interactions emphasize the importance of understanding the broader context of human evolution, where multiple hominin species influenced each other's development and survival. The diverse and overlapping habitats of these species created opportunities for both competition and cooperation, driving the evolutionary innovations that ultimately shaped the course of human history. The study of these interactions provides valuable insights into the adaptive strategies, technological advancements, and social behaviors that characterized the Pleistocene epoch, offering a deeper understanding of the evolutionary processes that have defined our lineage.

Animals Neanderthals Hunted:

Neanderthals were skilled hunters who adapted their strategies to the diverse environments they inhabited. In the temperate forests and plains of Europe, Neanderthals hunted a variety of large herbivores such as deer, horses, and aurochs, which provided substantial meat, hides, and bones essential for their survival. They employed sophisticated hunting techniques, including the use of thrusting spears and cooperative hunting strategies, to take down these formidable creatures. Additionally, they hunted smaller animals such as wild boar, rabbits, and birds, which supplemented their diet and provided additional resources. The presence of various animal bones in Neanderthal sites indicates their ability to hunt and process game efficiently. These hunts were often complex and involved a high level of social organization, demonstrating their ability to plan and execute coordinated attacks on large prey. The reliance on such game not only provided essential nutrients but also allowed Neanderthals to thrive in the resource-rich environments of prehistoric Europe. Their knowledge of animal behavior and migration patterns was crucial for successful hunts, ensuring a steady supply of food and materials needed for survival. The variety of prey also included beavers and badgers, indicating their ability to hunt and trap smaller mammals in these regions.

In the Mediterranean regions and the Middle East, Neanderthals adapted to hunting smaller game such as gazelles, wild goats, and horses. This required different tactics, including ambush techniques and possibly traps to capture more agile prey. The varied landscape, with its mix of rocky terrain, forests, and open plains, presented unique challenges that Neanderthals met with ingenuity and adaptability. These animals were a crucial part of the Neanderthal diet, providing necessary nutrition in a challenging environment where larger prey was less abundant. Additionally, Neanderthals hunted other animals such as birds, tortoises, and even fish, showcasing their ability to exploit a wide range of food sources. The hunting of smaller game necessitated a broader range of skills and tools, highlighting the versatility of Neanderthal hunting strategies. This adaptability allowed them to exploit a wide range of environments and resources, showcasing their ability to survive and flourish in diverse conditions. Their use of local materials to create effective hunting tools and their understanding of the regional fauna's habits were key to their success in these areas. Evidence of marine resource use, such as shellfish and sea mammals, further demonstrates their ability to adapt their diet to available resources in coastal regions.

In colder northern regions, Neanderthals hunted large herbivores such as reindeer, bison, woolly rhinoceroses, and mammoths, which were abundant in the open tundra and taiga ecosystems. These hunts required endurance and knowledge of migratory patterns, demonstrating Neanderthals' deep understanding of their environment. Mammoths, in particular, were significant as they provided large quantities of meat, hides, and bones, essential for making tools and constructing shelters. The harsh climatic conditions of the north demanded exceptional resilience and physical strength, as well as sophisticated hunting techniques to track and capture fast-moving and often elusive prey. The ability to exploit these large animals was vital for their sustenance, as the meat, hides, and bones provided essential resources for food, clothing, and tools. Neanderthals also hunted smaller animals such as Arctic hares and birds, which were more readily available during certain seasons. In addition to these prey, they likely hunted smaller carnivores like foxes and wolves, utilizing their pelts for warmth. Hunting these large and dangerous animals often required large groups and significant physical exertion, including running and strategic planning. The diversity of prey across different regions underscores Neanderthals' adaptability and proficiency in hunting, enabling them to thrive in varied climates and landscapes. The Neanderthals' capacity to adapt their hunting strategies to different environments highlights their evolutionary success and their role as apex predators within their ecosystems. Their innovative approaches to hunting and resource use were central to their resilience and long-term survival as a species. The evidence of fishing and scavenging from predator kills further illustrates their opportunistic and resourceful nature, ensuring they maximized all available resources in their environment. It is fascinating to consider that, as a species, Neanderthals, like all apes, were not inherently built for hunting large game or fighting with beasts, yet they developed remarkable skills and strategies to thrive in their environments.

Animals That Hunted Neanderthals:

While Neanderthals were formidable hunters, they also faced significant threats from various predators in their environments. In Europe, large carnivores such as cave lions, hyenas, and bears posed a constant danger. Cave lions, which were larger than modern lions, roamed the open plains and dense forests, preying on large herbivores that Neanderthals also hunted. These powerful predators could easily overpower a Neanderthal, leading to deadly encounters. Hyenas, known for their strong jaws and scavenging behavior, often competed with Neanderthals for food, sometimes attacking them to claim their kills. Cave bears, which could reach sizes of up to 3.5 meters (11.5 feet) in length and weigh over 1,000 kilograms (2,200 pounds), were another significant threat. These massive bears often inhabited the same caves Neanderthals used for shelter, leading to potentially deadly confrontations. Fossil evidence shows signs of predator-inflicted wounds on Neanderthal bones, indicating that they were sometimes hunted by these fierce animals. In the open plains and forests, Neanderthals had to be constantly vigilant against these threats, employing strategies to avoid encounters and protect their groups. The dense forests and rugged landscapes of Europe provided ample hiding spots for predators, making surprise attacks a constant risk. Neanderthals likely developed sophisticated strategies to detect and deter these predators, such as choosing high-ground campsites and using fire to ward off nocturnal hunters. Their ability to coexist with such formidable predators highlights their resilience and adaptability, showcasing their capacity to navigate and survive in predator-rich environments. The presence of large packs of wolves and saber-toothed cats added to the peril, requiring Neanderthals to maintain a heightened state of awareness and readiness to defend themselves and their communities.

In the Middle Eastern and Mediterranean regions, Neanderthals faced dangers from large cats like leopards and other carnivores adapted to these environments. These predators, adept at stalking and ambushing their prey, posed a significant threat to Neanderthal safety. Leopards, in particular, were known for their stealth and agility, making them formidable adversaries. Neanderthals had to be especially cautious in rocky and densely vegetated areas where leopards could easily conceal themselves. In addition to leopards, other predators such as jackals and hyenas also posed threats. The ability to defend against these predators and secure safe habitats was crucial for their survival. Neanderthals employed various defensive strategies, including the use of natural shelters like caves and rock overhangs, which offered protection from sudden attacks. Fire played a pivotal role in their defense strategy, not only providing warmth and light but also serving as a deterrent against nocturnal predators. The constant threat from these predators required Neanderthals to develop effective defensive measures and maintain a high level of vigilance, ensuring the safety of their groups and the continuity of their communities. The harsh and arid landscapes of the Middle East demanded exceptional adaptability and resourcefulness, as Neanderthals navigated these environments while avoiding dangerous predators.

In colder northern regions, Neanderthals contended with apex predators like cave bears and wolves. Neanderthals had to balance the need for shelter with the risk of encountering these formidable animals. The harsh climatic conditions and limited food resources in these regions intensified the competition between Neanderthals and predators. Wolves, often hunting in packs, posed a relentless threat, capable of overpowering isolated individuals or small groups. Neanderthals likely developed strategies to defend against these coordinated attacks, including creating barriers at cave entrances and establishing lookout points. The ability to repel these predators and maintain control over vital resources was essential for their survival. The interaction with these apex predators highlights the challenging and dangerous environments Neanderthals inhabited, underscoring their ingenuity and adaptability. The constant need to defend themselves against powerful predators contributed to the development of their strategic thinking and collaborative efforts, essential traits for their survival in the Pleistocene epoch. The Neanderthals' ability to survive in such harsh conditions, facing formidable predators and enduring extreme weather, showcases their exceptional resilience and adaptability as a species.

Other Animals:

Apart from those animals, Neanderthals coexisted with a variety of other unique and curious species. The Ice Age megafauna included fascinating creatures such as the short-faced bear and the saber-toothed cat. The short-faced bear, one of the largest and most powerful predators of the time, could stand up to 12 feet tall on its hind legs and weigh up to 1,800 pounds, posing a significant threat to Neanderthals. The saber-toothed cat, with its impressive canine teeth, was another formidable predator that coexisted with Neanderthals, adding to the danger in their environment. Additionally, Neanderthals shared their habitats with the aurochs, an ancestor of modern cattle, and the giant deer, also known as the Irish elk, which had enormous antlers that could span up to 3.5 meters (11.5 feet). The cave hyena, an opportunistic predator, often competed with Neanderthals for prey and was not shy about stealing their hard-earned kills. Other intriguing animals included the woolly rhinoceros, which roamed the colder climates alongside mammoths. These interactions with a wide range of animal species highlight the rich biodiversity of the Pleistocene epoch and the complex ecological web in which Neanderthals lived. The coexistence with such a diverse array of fauna underscores the adaptability and resourcefulness of Neanderthals as they navigated a world teeming with both opportunities and dangers.

In conclusion, Neanderthals demonstrated remarkable adaptability and resilience in their interactions with the animal world. They hunted and fought animals much larger and more formidable than themselves, employing sophisticated techniques and tools. From the mammoths and woolly rhinoceroses of the colder climates to the cave lions and short-faced bears of the more temperate regions, Neanderthals faced numerous challenges. Their ability to hunt large game and defend themselves against fierce predators highlights their ingenuity and advanced cognitive abilities. This complex relationship with the animal kingdom played a crucial role in their survival and evolutionary success, showcasing their unique position in the Pleistocene ecosystem.

CHAPTER 8:

A STORY: THE BEAST IN THE COLD

Introduction:

This chapter presents a fictional yet realistic story of a day in the life of a Neanderthal group living approximately 47,000 years ago near the Hohle Fels cave in the Swabian Jura region of Baden-Württemberg, Germany. This story aims to provide an immersive experience into the daily routines, challenges, and social interactions of the Neanderthals, based on current anthropological and archaeological understanding of their era and lifestyle.

Baden-Württemberg In Germany, 45,025 BCE

The landscape outside the Hohle Fels cave was a frozen tableau, with snow-covered ground stretching as far as the eye could see. The sky was overcast, casting a dull, gray light over the rugged terrain of the Swabian Jura. Icy winds howled through the valleys, carrying the chill of the Pleistocene epoch and sending shivers through any creature caught in its path. The forest, once lush and teeming with life, now stood as a stark, skeletal reminder of the harsh winter. Inside the cave, the atmosphere was warmer and filled with the flickering glow of a crackling fire. The flames danced on the rough stone walls, casting elongated shadows of the four Neanderthals huddled around it. This small group, part of a larger clan, sought refuge from the biting cold within this ancient shelter. The air was thick with the smell of burning wood and cooking meat, providing a stark contrast to the biting cold just outside the cave entrance. The cave's interior was a mix of stone and earth, with nooks and crannies that provided additional shelter and storage for their meager belongings. Bones and tools, evidence of previous meals and hard work, lay scattered around, telling silent stories of their daily struggles and survival. The cave itself was both a haven and a fortress, protecting them from the harsh elements and the predators that roamed the icy wilderness.

Nicki and Dallas, both 23 years old, sat close to the fire, their strong and sturdy frames silhouetted against the warm glow. They were busily tending to a freshly cooked rabbit, its aroma mingling with the scent of burning wood and adding a moment of comfort to their otherwise harsh existence. The males, Joe, 20, and Darwin, 29, were similarly built, their muscular bodies a testament to the rigorous demands of their environment. As they ate, they exchanged smiles and laughs, finding a brief respite from their daily hardships. The rabbit, a modest meal, was shared among them with a sense of camaraderie and necessity. Their faces, illuminated by the firelight, showed the wear and resilience of beings well-suited to their environment. The fire's warmth was a precious commodity, offering both physical comfort and a sense of security against the dark, cold world outside. Their tools and weapons, meticulously crafted from stone and bone, lay within reach, ready to be used at a moment's notice. Just as they were finishing their meal, a sudden, powerful roar pierced the cold air outside the cave, sending a shiver down their spines. The sound reverberated through the cavernous space. The Neanderthals froze, their instincts waking as they listened intently to the ominous sound outside.

Chapter 2: The Encounter:

 Nicki, Dallas, Joe, and Darwin exchanged tense glances as the roar faded into the cold silence of the night. Armed with two spears each, they cautiously made their way out of the cave to investigate. The icy wind bit at their faces as they stepped into the bleak landscape, their breaths visible in the frigid air. The moon cast a pale light, illuminating the snow-covered ground and the dense forest beyond. Every shadow seemed to move, and every sound heightened their senses. They scanned the area, alert for any sign of danger, but found nothing. The silence was almost deafening, broken only by the distant howling of the wind through the trees. The four Neanderthals stood in the snow, their eyes searching the darkness for any hint of movement. Their muscles were tense, and their grips on the spears were firm, ready to react to the slightest sign of danger. The chill of the night seeped into their bones, but their determination kept them moving forward. The cold air stung their lungs with each breath, a harsh reminder of the unforgiving environment they called home. Snow crunched under their feet as they moved cautiously, each step deliberate and measured. The shadows of the forest loomed menacingly, creating an eerie backdrop to their tense exploration.

 Just as they turned to head back into the relative safety of the cave, a massive cave bear emerged from the shadows, blocking their entrance. The bear, weighing around a ton, was an imposing sight, its thick fur bristling in the cold air. Its eyes glowed with a predatory intensity, and its massive paws left deep prints in the snow. The Neanderthals froze for a moment, the sheer size of the beast rendering them momentarily speechless. Dallas and Joe, driven by instinct, immediately hurled their spears at the beast. The spears struck the bear in the shoulder, eliciting a furious roar that echoed through the valley. The bear's eyes glowed with rage as it advanced towards them, each step more deliberate and menacing than the last. Darwin and Nicki stood ready, their spears poised in a defensive position, their breaths coming in rapid, visible puffs. The bear's growls reverberated through the night air, sending a new wave of fear through the Neanderthals. The ground seemed to tremble under its massive weight. Nicki, her instincts taking over, threw her second spear with all her strength, aiming for the beast's chest. The spear found its mark, but the bear only grew more furious, its eyes burning with fury. Dallas and Joe quickly retreated, joining Darwin and Nicki in a tight defensive formation. The firelight flickered inside the cave, casting an eerie glow on the bear's massive form and the determined faces of the Neanderthals. They knew they were facing a battle for survival, with the odds heavily stacked against them.

The bear, now enraged and wounded, advanced towards them, its growls resonating through the night air. The Neanderthals braced themselves, their hearts pounding in their chests. Dallas and Joe readied their spears, their hands steady despite the adrenaline coursing through their veins. The beast moved forward, its massive form blocking the light from the cave, casting the Neanderthals in its dark shadow. In a desperate move, Nicki threw her spear once more, aiming for the beast's chest. The spear found its mark, but the bear only grew more enraged. It roared, the sound a mix of pain and fury. The bear's breath was visible in the cold air, its eyes burning with fury as it prepared to charge. The Neanderthals knew they couldn't withstand a direct assault from the enraged animal, so they made a split-second decision to retreat into the wilderness. They turned and ran, the howling wind and falling snow obscuring their vision. The storm intensified, snow swirling around them, making it difficult to see or hear. After what felt like an eternity, but was only a few minutes, they stopped to catch their breath, their lungs burning from the exertion and cold air. They looked at each other, their eyes wide with fear and determination, knowing they had to stay alert. Suddenly, without warning, the bear lunged out of the storm, its massive body slamming into Nicki. The force of the attack was overwhelming, and before the others could react, the bear's powerful jaws tore into her, ending her life in an instant.

Chapter 3: The Aftermath:

The three remaining Neanderthals stood in stunned silence, looking at Nicki's lifeless body. The bear, still thrashing in its final moments, continued to maul her even as her life had already ebbed away. Grief and rage surged through them, driving them into action. With a unified, primal scream, they lunged at the bear, their spears striking repeatedly. Joe and Dallas stabbed at its sides, each blow fueled by a mixture of fear, anger, and desperation. Darwin, with a final surge of strength, aimed for the bear's throat, driving his spear deep into its flesh. The beast let out a final, agonized roar before collapsing to the ground, its massive body still at last.

The storm outside began to ease, the howling wind gradually dying down to a gentle whisper. Snowflakes fell softly, blanketing the landscape in a serene, deceptive calm. The Neanderthals, their breaths heavy and visible in the cold air, stood over the bear's lifeless form, their hands and bodies trembling from the exertion and adrenaline. They were exhausted, their muscles aching from the fight, but the immediate danger had passed.

As the storm subsided, they made their way back to the cave, carrying Nicki's body with them. Their movements were slow and deliberate, each step a struggle against the emotional and physical toll of the battle. Inside the cave, the rest of their clan awaited them, worry etched on their faces. When they saw Nicki's lifeless form, a wave of sorrow swept through the group. They gathered around, offering what comfort they could, their faces reflecting the shared grief of losing one of their own.

The fire in the cave burned low, casting a somber glow on the scene. The warmth that had once provided comfort now seemed insufficient against the cold reality of their loss. The clan members murmured softly to each other, their voices filled with sadness and respect for the fallen. They knew that life in their harsh world was always precarious, but each loss felt deeply personal, a reminder of their own fragility.

As night fell, they began the solemn task of preparing Nicki for burial. They chose a spot near the entrance of the cave, where the ground was soft enough to dig. The entire clan participated, their movements a quiet testament to their collective grief and resilience. They worked in silence, their hearts heavy with the weight of their loss. The firelight flickered, casting long shadows on the cave walls, as they prepared to lay Nicki to rest.

In the end, as they gathered around her final resting place, they reflected on the fragility of life and the strength of their bonds. They knew that despite the dangers and hardships they faced, their unity and resilience would carry them forward.

Chapter 4: ChaFarewell and Remembrance:

The cold morning light filtered through the entrance of the cave as the Neanderthals gathered to lay Nicki to rest. Her body was carefully wrapped in animal hides, a final act of care from her clan. The chosen burial spot near the entrance of the cave was marked by a simple mound of freshly dug earth. The air was thick with sorrow, and the quiet sounds of their labor were punctuated by the soft cries of mourning. As they placed her in the ground, the gravity of their loss settled heavily upon them.

Each member of the clan took a moment to say their silent goodbyes. Tears streamed down their faces, mingling with the dirt and snow as they gently covered her body with earth. Dallas, her closest companion, placed a delicate flower on the grave, its bright color a stark contrast to the gray landscape. Joe laid Nicki's final spear beside her, the weapon that had served her so well in life now resting with her in death. It was a symbol of her strength and the battles she had fought alongside them.

Darwin, usually stoic, let his grief show as he knelt by the grave, tears mingling with the snow. The others followed suit, their sobs a raw, unfiltered expression of the pain they felt. The burial was not just a farewell to Nicki but a poignant reminder of the fragility of their existence. The fire in the cave seemed a distant warmth now, as the cold reality of their loss took hold.

Once the burial was complete, the clan made their way back to the cave. The journey was somber, each step heavy with the weight of their grief. Inside, the fire burned low, casting a warm glow on the stone walls. The familiar scents of smoke and charred wood filled the air, bringing a semblance of normalcy to their world.

In a gesture of remembrance, they decided to create a lasting tribute to Nicki. Using red ochre and their hands, they began to make handprints on the cave wall. Each member pressed their right hand against the stone, leaving behind a mark that symbolized their bond and their shared loss. The wall, now adorned with handprints, became a canvas of memory, a way to honor Nicki's life and her place within the clan.

Dallas, with tears still in her eyes, added the final touch. She carefully placed Nicki's handprint among the others, her own hand shaking as she pressed it against the cold stone. The act was both cathartic and heartbreaking, a final goodbye that would remain etched in the cave for generations to come.

As they stood back and looked at the wall, a sense of quiet solidarity settled over them. The handprints, bathed in the soft glow of the fire, served as a poignant reminder of their fallen companion. It was a simple yet powerful tribute, a way to keep Nicki's memory alive in the place that had been their sanctuary.
The chapter of their lives marked by this loss was a harsh reminder of the world they lived in. But it also underscored their resilience and the strength of their bonds. As the fire crackled and the wind howled outside, the Neanderthals found comfort

in their shared memories and the enduring spirit of their clan. They knew that, despite the pain, they would continue to face the challenges of their world together, carrying Nicki's memory with them into the future.

CHAPTER 9:

WHAT IF THEY WERE ALIVE TODAY

Understanding Neanderthals and their differences from Homo sapiens is a complex task, filled with nuances and uncertainties. While modern science provides us with incredible insights into their biology, intelligence, and capabilities, it's important to remember that these interpretations are based on the best available evidence and may not be entirely accurate. This chapter explores whether early Homo sapiens would have noticed significant differences between themselves and Neanderthals, compares the intelligence of Neanderthals to modern humans, and discusses the tasks Neanderthals might be able to perform in today's world.

Would We Notice the Difference?:

Early Homo sapiens, upon encountering Neanderthals, likely perceived them as different but not entirely alien. Much like how people from different regions of the world recognize physical differences today, early humans might have noticed the Neanderthals' robust build, prominent brow ridges, and larger noses. However, these differences were probably seen as variations within the human spectrum rather than markers of a distinct species. The similarities in their tool-making techniques, social structures, and interbreeding suggest that early Homo sapiens and Neanderthals might have seen each other as part of the same extended family, albeit with notable physical variations. Just as modern Chinese people might notice differences in appearance when compared to Europeans, early humans likely viewed Neanderthals through a similar lens, recognizing physical differences but also acknowledging shared traits and behaviors.

The close proximity of their cultures likely facilitated interaction and exchange. The sharing of tools, techniques, and possibly even members of each group would have blurred the lines further. Today, with advanced scientific tools, we can identify genetic markers that clearly distinguish Neanderthals from modern humans. However, on a superficial level, many of the differences might still be subtle. For instance, while a trained anthropologist could identify a Neanderthal based on skeletal remains or specific physical features, an average person might only notice differences in build and facial structure. In everyday interactions, especially in environments where cultural and social behaviors dominate, these physical differences might seem less significant. The similarities in their capabilities and lifestyles would have likely overshadowed the distinctions, emphasizing their shared humanity rather than their differences.

How Smart Were They Compared to Us?:

Comparing the intelligence of Neanderthals to modern humans is a challenging endeavor, as intelligence encompasses a wide range of abilities, including problem-solving, social interaction, and cultural innovation. Neanderthals demonstrated remarkable cognitive abilities, evident in their sophisticated tool-making, use of fire, and possible symbolic behavior. They created and used tools that were specialized and effective, indicating advanced planning and understanding of their environment. Additionally, archaeological evidence suggests that Neanderthals may have had some form of language, as well as the capacity for symbolic thought, as seen in the creation of personal ornaments and cave art.

While Neanderthals were undoubtedly intelligent, their cognitive strengths might have differed from those of modern humans. They excelled in spatial awareness and physical problem-solving, crucial for their survival in harsh environments. Modern humans, on the other hand, have developed advanced abstract thinking, allowing for complex language, art, and technology. The differences in brain structure between Neanderthals and Homo sapiens might explain these cognitive variations. Neanderthals had larger occipital lobes, suggesting superior visual processing abilities, while Homo sapiens have more developed parietal lobes, associated with complex social interactions and abstract thought. These differences do not necessarily imply that one species was smarter than the other but rather that they were adapted to their specific environments and challenges in unique ways. We know that Neanderthals were close to us in many aspects and exhibited intelligence in areas such as healing and survival strategies. This means we cannot definitively measure how smart they were compared to us, but it is clear they were highly intelligent and well-adapted to their environment.

Tasks They Could Perform Today and Those They Could Not:

If Neanderthals were suddenly brought into today's world, there are several tasks they could likely perform successfully, especially those requiring physical strength and spatial awareness. Jobs in construction, agriculture, and certain types of manual labor would suit their robust physiques and practical problem-solving skills. Their ability to create and use tools effectively suggests that they could adapt to modern machinery and equipment with appropriate training. Moreover, their social structures and cooperative behavior indicate that they could work well in team settings, relying on their inherent sense of community and mutual support.

However, there would be significant challenges in tasks requiring advanced abstract thinking, technological proficiency, and modern communication skills. The rapid pace of technological change and the reliance on digital tools would pose a considerable barrier. Tasks that require complex language skills, such as those in education, administration, or any field involving extensive communication, might be difficult for Neanderthals to master. Additionally, the modern workplace's social and cultural nuances, including etiquette and interpersonal dynamics, could present challenges. While Neanderthals were undoubtedly intelligent and capable, the cognitive differences and lack of exposure to modern society's complexities would limit their ability to perform certain tasks that require high levels of abstract reasoning and technological adeptness.

Discussing the intelligence of Neanderthals seriously is still in its early stages. New techniques and methods in archaeology, anthropology, and genetics are continually emerging, providing fresh insights and challenging our understanding of these ancient humans. As these technologies advance, we will likely gain a more nuanced and accurate picture of Neanderthal intelligence and their capabilities, helping us to appreciate the full extent of their cognitive abilities.

CHAPTER 10:
ROLE IN HUMAN EVOLUTION

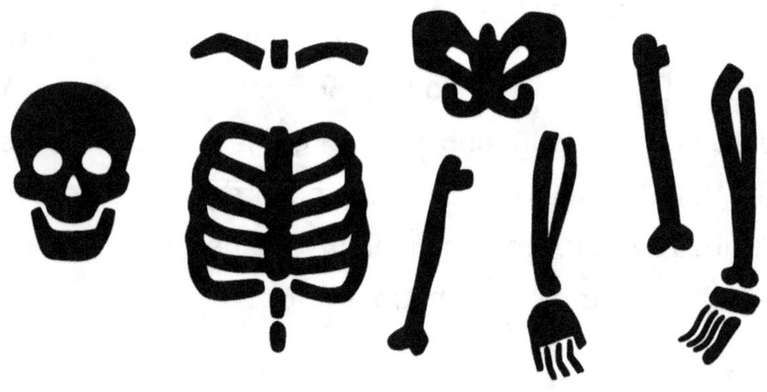

The Neanderthals, our closest ancient relatives, left an indelible mark on the history of human evolution. Their legacy includes technological innovations, geographic dispersal and adaptation, biological and anatomical changes, brain size and intelligence, social structure and behavior, interbreeding and genetic legacy, and their cultural and cognitive contributions. By exploring these areas, we can gain a deeper understanding of how Neanderthals have shaped our own species and the world we live in today.

Technological Innovations:

Neanderthals were skilled toolmakers, and their technological innovations played a crucial role in their survival and adaptation to diverse environments. They developed the Mousterian tool industry, characterized by flake tools made from prepared cores, which demonstrated advanced planning and understanding of material properties. These tools included scrapers, points, and knives, which were used for hunting, butchering, and processing animal hides. Neanderthals also created hafted tools by attaching stone points to wooden shafts, increasing the efficiency and effectiveness of their weapons. Additionally, evidence suggests that they utilized fire not only for warmth and cooking but also for tool-making, as they heat-treated flint to improve its flaking properties. These technological advancements highlight the Neanderthals' ability to innovate and adapt their tools to meet the demands of their environment, showcasing their resourcefulness and cognitive capabilities.

Neanderthals' innovations extended beyond tools. They demonstrated the ability to create and use adhesives, such as pitch derived from birch bark, to secure stone tools to wooden handles. This process required knowledge of temperature control and material properties, indicating sophisticated cognitive skills. Moreover, the discovery of bone tools and possible musical instruments, such as the Divje Babe flute, suggests that Neanderthals engaged in complex behaviors that extended into cultural and symbolic realms. These technological and cultural advancements underscore the Neanderthals' intellectual capabilities and their significant contributions to the broader narrative of human evolution.

Geographic Dispersal and Adaptation:

Neanderthals inhabited a wide range of environments across Europe and western Asia, adapting to diverse climates and landscapes. Their geographic dispersal was extensive, from the Atlantic coasts of Europe to the western reaches of Siberia and from the Mediterranean regions to the colder northern latitudes. This vast range of habitats required Neanderthals to develop a variety of adaptive strategies to survive. In the colder climates, they built sturdy shelters, crafted warm clothing from animal hides, and relied heavily on hunting large game such as mammoths and reindeer. In more temperate regions, they adapted their diet to include a greater variety of plant foods and smaller game. The ability to thrive in such diverse environments demonstrates the Neanderthals' remarkable adaptability and resilience. Their geographic dispersal also facilitated cultural exchanges with other hominin species, contributing to their evolutionary success.

The diversity of environments inhabited by Neanderthals required them to be highly adaptable. In the Mediterranean regions, they exploited coastal resources, including shellfish and marine mammals, demonstrating their ability to utilize various ecological niches. In contrast, Neanderthals in the steppe and tundra regions of Europe and Asia had to contend with extreme cold and limited resources, which necessitated a focus on large game hunting and efficient use of available materials. The presence of Neanderthal remains in caves and open-air sites indicates their flexibility in choosing habitats that provided both shelter and access to resources. This geographic diversity not only highlights their adaptability but also their ability to interact with and adapt to different hominin populations, leading to a rich tapestry of cultural and genetic exchange.

Biological and Anatomical Changes:

The Neanderthals exhibited distinct biological and anatomical features that set them apart from modern humans. They had a robust build, with thick bones, broad shoulders, and barrel-shaped chests, which provided the physical strength necessary for their demanding lifestyle. Their skulls were characterized by prominent brow ridges, a large nose, and a forward-projecting face, adaptations that helped them survive in cold environments by warming and humidifying the air they breathed. Neanderthals also had shorter limbs and stockier bodies compared to modern humans, reducing heat loss and conserving energy in frigid climates. These anatomical changes were crucial for their survival, enabling them to endure the harsh conditions of the Ice Age.

In addition to their robust build, Neanderthals exhibited significant muscular development, which is evident from the muscle attachment sites on their bones. This muscularity suggests they were capable of great physical strength and endurance, necessary for their survival activities, such as hunting large game and constructing shelters. Neanderthals also had larger cranial capacities than modern humans, suggesting a complex and well-developed brain structure, but bigger does not necessarily mean smarter. Their teeth and jawbones were robust, indicating a diet that included tough, fibrous foods and possibly the use of their teeth as tools. Neanderthals were way stronger than us, and in a one-on-one physical confrontation, they would likely always win. These biological and anatomical features not only reflect their adaptation to the environment but also their ability to innovate and survive in challenging conditions.

Social Structure and Behavior:

Neanderthals exhibited complex social structures and behaviors that were crucial for their survival. They lived in small, close-knit groups that relied on cooperation and mutual support. Evidence from burial sites suggests that they cared for their sick and injured, indicating a strong sense of community and empathy. Neanderthals also demonstrated advanced medical knowledge, as seen in the use of medicinal plants and the setting of broken bones. Their social interactions likely included a form of communication, possibly even language, which would have facilitated cooperation and the sharing of knowledge. The presence of symbolic artifacts, such as personal ornaments and cave art, suggests that Neanderthals engaged in cultural and symbolic behaviors, further highlighting their cognitive complexity. Importantly, they buried their dead, often with care and possibly with ritualistic elements, which underscores their social bonds and spiritual beliefs.

The social structures of Neanderthals were likely similar to those of early Homo sapiens, with group sizes varying depending on the availability of resources and environmental conditions. They exhibited a division of labor, with different members of the group taking on specific roles, such as hunting, gathering, and childcare. This division of labor would have increased their efficiency and survival chances. Neanderthals also engaged in complex hunting strategies that required cooperation and planning, further emphasizing their social cohesion. Their ability to form strong social bonds and work together as a unit was a key factor in their success and adaptability. The practice of burying their dead, including sometimes placing grave goods with the deceased, further illustrates their complex social and emotional lives, as well as their cognitive sophistication.

Interbreeding and Genetic Legacy:

Today, most modern humans carry a small but significant genetic legacy from Neanderthals. Genetic studies have revealed that most of the populations have between 1% and 2% Neanderthal DNA, indicating that interbreeding occurred when Homo sapiens and Neanderthals coexisted in Europe and Asia. This genetic legacy has had various impacts on modern humans, influencing traits such as immune system responses, skin pigmentation, and even susceptibility to certain diseases.

The presence of Neanderthal DNA in modern humans highlights the close evolutionary relationship between the two species and the dynamic interactions that shaped our genetic heritage. This interbreeding underscores the complexity of human evolution and the ways in which Neanderthals have contributed to the genetic diversity and adaptability of contemporary human populations.

The discovery of Neanderthal DNA in modern humans has provided valuable insights into the evolutionary history of our species. It has revealed the complexity of human evolution, characterized by periods of interbreeding and gene flow between different hominin populations. This genetic exchange not only contributed to the diversity of modern human populations but also provided adaptive advantages that enhanced survival in different environments. For instance, genes inherited from Neanderthals have been linked to adaptations to cold climates and resistance to certain pathogens. The study of Neanderthal genetics continues to uncover new aspects of their legacy, deepening our understanding of their role in shaping the human genome.

Cultural and Cognitive Contributions:

Neanderthals made significant cultural and cognitive contributions that have enriched our understanding of human evolution. They created symbolic artifacts, such as beads made from animal teeth and shells, which were likely used for decorative or symbolic purposes. The discovery of cave art attributed to Neanderthals, such as the paintings in Spain, suggests that they engaged in symbolic thought and had an appreciation for aesthetics. Neanderthals also demonstrated the ability to create and use complex tools, indicating advanced planning and problem-solving skills. Their cultural practices, such as the burial of their dead with grave goods, reflect a deep sense of community and possibly even spiritual beliefs.

The cognitive abilities of Neanderthals are further highlighted by their ability to adapt to changing environments and innovate in their tool-making techniques. The presence of musical instruments, such as the Divje Babe flute, suggests that they engaged in musical activities, adding another dimension to their cultural repertoire. These cultural and cognitive contributions provide a richer and more nuanced understanding of Neanderthals, challenging earlier perceptions of them as less advanced than modern humans. Instead, they emerge as a species with complex behaviors and intellectual capabilities that were crucial for their survival and adaptation.

Our Closest Cousin:

Neanderthals, as our closest ancient relatives, hold a special place in the story of human evolution. Their legacy is woven into the fabric of modern human populations, through both genetic inheritance and shared cultural practices. The study of Neanderthals provides valuable insights into the evolutionary processes that have shaped our species, highlighting the importance of adaptation, innovation, and social cohesion. As we continue to uncover new information about Neanderthals, we gain a deeper appreciation for their contributions to the human story and their enduring impact on our understanding of what it means to be human.

The legacy of Neanderthals is multifaceted and profound, encompassing technological innovations, geographic adaptability, biological and anatomical changes, cognitive and cultural contributions, and a lasting genetic impact on modern humans. As we continue to explore and understand their legacy, we are reminded of the interconnectedness of all human species and the shared journey of evolution. The study of Neanderthals not only enriches our knowledge of the past but also provides valuable perspectives on the resilience, adaptability, and ingenuity that define the human experience.

CHAPTER II:
HOW THEY BECAME EXTINCT

The extinction of Neanderthals remains one of the most intriguing and debated topics in paleoanthropology. Despite their advanced cognitive abilities, complex social structures, and adaptability to diverse environments, Neanderthals disappeared around 40,000 years ago, leaving Homo sapiens as the sole surviving human species. Several theories attempt to explain their extinction, each highlighting different factors that may have contributed to their demise. One prominent theory suggests that competition with modern humans played a significant role. As Homo sapiens migrated into Neanderthal territories, they brought with them what might have been advanced technologies, more efficient hunting strategies, and possibly better social cohesion, which may have given them a competitive edge. The introduction of new diseases by Homo sapiens, to which Neanderthals had no immunity, could have further exacerbated their decline.

Another factor to consider is the Neanderthals' relatively small and isolated populations. Although they had a wide geographic range across Europe and western Asia, their population density was much lower than that of contemporary Homo sapiens. Estimates suggest that Neanderthal populations were about ten times smaller than those of Homo sapiens during their coexistence. This low population density would have made Neanderthals more vulnerable to environmental changes, resource scarcity, and genetic bottlenecks. Small, scattered groups would have had difficulty sustaining themselves and recovering from population declines caused by disease, climate fluctuations, or interspecies competition. Additionally, their smaller populations might have led to reduced genetic diversity, making it harder for Neanderthals to adapt to changing environments and new challenges.

Climate change during the last Ice Age also likely played a crucial role in the Neanderthals' extinction. The rapid and severe climatic shifts drastically altered the ecosystems that Neanderthals depended on for survival, impacting the availability of food, water, and shelter. As temperatures plummeted and glacial landscapes expanded, lush forests and grasslands were replaced by barren tundra and ice, forcing Neanderthals to adapt quickly to a deteriorating environment. The animals they hunted became scarce, further straining their ability to secure sufficient nutrition. Neanderthals faced increased difficulty in finding food and suitable shelter, as their robust bodies required substantial caloric intake. In contrast, Homo sapiens, with their more diverse dietary practices, could exploit a broader range of food sources, including plants, small game, and marine resources. Modern humans developed advanced tools and weapons, such as bone needles for sewing warm clothing and long-range hunting weapons, allowing them to thrive in diverse environments. Their ability to innovate and create effective survival strategies gave Homo sapiens a significant advantage in adapting to the rapidly changing climate. The ability of modern humans to form larger, more stable communities provided a buffer against the harsh climate, whereas Neanderthal groups, already small and isolated, struggled to cope. Larger communities facilitated better sharing of resources, knowledge, and support, enhancing group survival. In contrast, Neanderthal populations faced isolation that hindered their ability to collaborate and innovate collectively, leading to genetic bottlenecks. The social structures of Homo sapiens, which included complex communication and sophisticated social hierarchies, likely helped in organizing large-scale efforts to secure food and build shelters, further increasing their chances of surviving through the worst climatic periods. The combined effects of climatic shifts, resource scarcity, and the superior adaptability of Homo sapiens created an environment where Neanderthals found it increasingly difficult to survive, leading to their eventual extinction.

Interbreeding between Neanderthals and Homo sapiens also played a role in their eventual disappearance, although not necessarily through direct competition or conflict. This interbreeding suggests a level of interaction and integration between the two species. However, as Homo sapiens became more dominant, Neanderthals may have been gradually absorbed into the larger human population. Over generations, the distinct Neanderthal identity could have faded as they interbred with and assimilated into the growing Homo sapiens communities. The presence of Neanderthal DNA in modern humans highlights the close evolutionary relationship between the two species and the dynamic interactions that shaped our genetic heritage. This interbreeding underscores the complexity of human evolution and the ways in which Neanderthals have contributed to the genetic diversity and adaptability of contemporary human populations.

The extinction of Neanderthals is likely the result of a combination of factors rather than a single cause. The interplay of competition with Homo sapiens, environmental pressures, small population sizes, and interbreeding created a complex scenario that led to their decline. Despite their extinction, Neanderthals left a lasting legacy through their genetic contributions to modern humans and the rich archaeological record that continues to shed light on their lives and capabilities. Their story is a testament to the intricate web of interactions and adaptations that characterize human evolution, reminding us of the resilience and adaptability that define our species.

In conclusion, 40,000 years ago, we lost our closest species, but they still live on within each of us. Their extinction marks a significant chapter in the history of human evolution, illustrating the dynamic and often precarious nature of existence. After their extinction, we were left alone, and for thousands of years, we thought we were always alone, but now we know we were not. The legacy of the Neanderthals endures in our DNA, our shared history, and the ongoing quest to unravel the mysteries of our past.

Conclusion

The story of the Neanderthals provides a profound insight into the resilience and adaptability that have characterized the human journey. Neanderthals were a species that demonstrated remarkable ingenuity and resourcefulness, creating sophisticated tools and developing complex social structures to thrive in diverse and often harsh environments. Their technological advancements, such as the development of the Mousterian tool industry, and their ability to adapt to a wide range of ecological niches highlight their cognitive and cultural sophistication. This narrative reveals the Neanderthals as a crucial part of our evolutionary history, showing that they were much more than a side branch of the human family tree.

The extinction of the Neanderthals around 40,000 years ago was a significant event in the tapestry of human evolution. Despite their impressive abilities and adaptations, they faced insurmountable challenges that led to their decline. The rapid climate changes of the last Ice Age drastically altered their habitats, making survival increasingly difficult. Additionally, competition with Homo sapiens, who brought new technologies and social structures, further strained Neanderthal populations. Their relatively small and isolated groups struggled to maintain genetic diversity and recover from environmental and competitive pressures. While interbreeding with Homo sapiens did occur, it likely contributed to their gradual assimilation and loss of distinct identity. These complex interactions underscore the multifaceted nature of their extinction.

As we reflect on the Neanderthals' journey, we gain valuable perspectives on the broader story of human evolution. Their legacy lives on, not only in the genetic traces found in modern human populations but also in the lessons they teach us about survival, adaptation, and innovation. The Neanderthals' ability to create and use tools, their development of social bonds and care for their communities, and their adaptability to changing environments all highlight traits that are fundamental to the human experience. Understanding their story enriches our appreciation of our own species' resilience and capacity for growth. As we continue to uncover more about the Neanderthals, we deepen our understanding of our shared past and the intricate web of connections that define human history. The legacy of the Neanderthals endures, reminding us of the profound and enduring connections we share with our ancient relatives.

The Next Book
"Homo Sapiens: The Dominant Species,"

As we draw near the end of our journey, it is important to reflect on the path we've taken. This book is the fifth in a six-part series that delves into the fascinating journey of our ancient ancestors. Each book has uncovered the mysteries and marvels of different hominin species, building a comprehensive picture of human evolution. From the early days of Homo habilis to the advanced capabilities of Neanderthals, each chapter has brought us closer to understanding the complexity and diversity of our lineage. This exploration has not only highlighted the unique attributes of each species but also underscored the interconnectedness of our evolutionary history.

But our journey into other Homo species ends here. All we have left to explore is ourselves. The next book, "Homo sapiens: The Dominant Species" will delve into our emergence and how we came to dominate the planet. We will explore critical milestones, such as our close encounters with extinction, the exodus from Africa, the dawn of agriculture, and the growth of our population over time. This book will also discuss the cultural, technological, and social advancements that have defined our species. Join us as we conclude this journey together, uncovering the story of how Homo sapiens evolved to become the species we are today.

Glossary of Terms

Anatomy:

- The study of the structure of organisms and their parts. In this book, it often refers to the physical characteristics of Neanderthals.

Anthropology:

- The study of humans, past and present. It encompasses several fields, including cultural, social, biological, and archaeological anthropology.

Archaeology:

- The study of human history and prehistory through the excavation and analysis of artifacts, fossils, and other physical remains.

Bipedalism:

- The ability to walk upright on two legs, a characteristic of all hominins including Neanderthals.

Cognitive Capabilities:

- The mental skills and abilities that Neanderthals possessed, including problem-solving, memory, and possibly language.

Cranial Capacity:

- The volume of the braincase, which in Neanderthals was larger on average than in modern humans.

Paleoanthropology:

- The branch of anthropology concerned with fossil hominids.

Pleistocene Epoch:

- The geological time period that lasted from about 2.6 million to 11,700 years ago, encompassing the time when Neanderthals lived.

Symbolic Behavior:

- Actions or artifacts that signify something beyond their literal meaning, such as art, ornaments, or burial practices.

Upper Paleolithic:

- The final phase of the Paleolithic period, characterized by the emergence of modern humans and the decline of Neanderthals.

References

Books:

"Masters of the Planet: The Search for Our Human Origins" by Ian Tattersall (St. Martin's Press)

"The Complete World of Human Evolution" by Chris Stringer and Peter Andrews (Thames & Hudson)

YouTube Channels: "North 02" & "PBS Eons"

Articles and Journals:

"Mum's a Neanderthal, Dad's a Denisovan: First Discovery of an Ancient-Human Hybrid" by Slon et al. (Nature)

www.ingramcontent.com/pod-product-compliance
Lightning Source LLC
Chambersburg PA
CBHW050803250726
48653CB00006B/2045